THE PAST BEFORE US

INDIGENOUS
PACIFICS

SERIES EDITORS

*Noelani Goodyear-Kaʻōpua
and April K. Henderson*

*FACING THE SPEARS OF CHANGE: THE LIFE
AND LEGACY OF JOHN PAPA ʻĪʻĪ*
Marie Alohalani Brown

*FOUND IN TRANSLATION: MANY MEANINGS
ON A NORTH AUSTRALIAN MISSION*
Laura Rademaker

THE PAST BEFORE US

Moʻokūʻauhau as Methodology

EDITED BY
NĀLANI WILSON-HOKOWHITU

UNIVERSITY OF HAWAIʻI PRESS
HONOLULU

24 23 22 21 20 19   6 5 4 3 2 1

Library of Congress Cataloging-in-Publication Data

Names: Wilson-Hokowhitu, Nalani, editor.
Title: The past before us : mookuauhau as methodology / edited by Nalani
Wilson-Hokowhitu.
Other titles: Past before us (2019) | Indigenous Pacifics.
Description: Honolulu : University of Hawaii Press, [2019] | Series:
Indigenous Pacifics | Includes bibliographical references and index.
Identifiers: LCCN 2018039778| ISBN 9780824873387 (cloth ; alk. paper) | ISBN
9780824873394 (pbk. ; alk. paper)
Subjects: LCSH: Hawaii—Civilization. | Hawaiians—Genealogy—Methodology. |
Knowledge, Theory of—Hawaii. | Hawaiian philosophy.
Classification: LCC DU624.5 .P37 2019 | DDC 996.9—dc23
LC record available at https://lccn.loc.gov/2018039778

University of Hawai'i Press books are printed on acid-free
paper and meet the guidelines for permanence and
durability of the Council on Library Resources.

Cover art: *Hina Sailing into the Moon* (2017), an original watercolor painting
by Nālani Wilson-Hokowhitu, depicts legendary voyager and navigator
Hina-faʻauru-vaʻa ("Hina the canoe pilot") and her transformation into
Hina-nui-te-araara ("Great Hina the watch woman"). The painting is a
visual interpretation of "sailing into the future, guided by the past."

CONTENTS

Foreword

Nearly two thousand years ago, our seafaring Polynesian ancestors left their homeland, navigating the ocean until they reached the archipelago known today as Hawai'i. As centuries passed, our language and culture evolved to the point that we became a distinct people—the 'Ōiwi (one of several descriptors for ourselves). Two critical points here bear reiterating. First, our islands shaped us physically, intellectually, and spiritually: our 'ike (knowledge, experience, perspective) is grounded in the realities of our island existence. Second, our culture has always been dynamic and thus always evolving. Crucially, past, present, and future are tightly woven in 'Ōiwi theory and practice. We adapt to whatever historical challenges we face so that we can continue to survive and thrive. As we look to the past for knowledge and inspiration on how to face the future, we are aware that we are tomorrow's ancestors, and future generations will look to us for guidance.

The concepts of continuity and relationality go together in 'Ōiwi thought: together, they form the kuamo'o (backbone) of Hawaiian culture, and they are fully encapsulated in the term *mo'okū'auhau*. In its narrowest sense, mo'okū'auhau, often translated as *genealogy*, refers to biological continuity and biological relationality. Significantly, 'Ōiwi perceive the world genealogically. We are part of a complex web of relationality in which everything in our native island world (land, sea, and sky, and all therein) are kin. This relationality is also spiritual for we are the younger human relatives of the other-than-human entities in our island world, many of whom we consider akua (deities). Noenoe Silva, in *The Power of the Steel-Tipped Pen: Reconstructing Native Hawaiian Intellectual History*, writes extensively about "moʻokūʻauhau consciousness," which is "an ethic and orientation to the world" (2017, 4). Indeed, moʻokūʻauhau is an apt philosophical construct for understanding other kinds of genealogies: conceptual (the worldview our ancestors bequeathed us); intellectual (knowledge and practices generated, learned, and transmitted); aesthetic (inherited ideas about what constitutes the good and beautiful, which are encapsulated in ʻŌiwi poetic devices); and power (inherited authority or capacity to effect change). These different kinds of moʻokūʻauhau—physical, intellectual, and spiritual—are necessary to our survival. We are more than the sum of our physical bodies—our language and our artistic-intellectual-spiritual traditions are critical to who we are as a people, and, as I have just explained, traditions have a genealogy.

It bears saying that everything we consider a tradition was once an innovation. Traditions come into being when the community finds a practice or a process useful or important enough to replicate, teach, and transmit across generations. Traditional practices and processes include how we construct canoes, carve drums, set up loʻi kalo (irrigated taro fields), dance hula, use our voice in chant, compose chants or moʻolelo, weave lau hala (pandanus leaves), and how we teach all of these. Significantly, innovations are rooted in tradition: small differences in traditional practices lead to new ways of doing things. Should an innovation on a tradition stray too far from what is considered acceptable, the community might refuse it. In short, ʻŌiwi are the judges of what is culturally significant for us, what should be conserved for posterity and prosperity, and when innovation is desirable or undesirable.

Here, I turn my considerations to the term *moʻo*, which provides an example of how our island environment can inspire theoretical constructs related to continuity and relevance. Mary Kawena Pukui, in *The Polynesian Family System of Ka-ʻu, Hawaiʻi* (1958), explains that the lizard's knobby backbone is a fitting simile for genealogical continuity. Moreover, lizards regrow their tails. Thus, the lizard's physicality stands for biological continuity. Indeed, *moʻo* means *lizard* and *series* or *succession*. There is good cause to suspect that our island moʻo (geckos and skinks) inspired several (if not all) meanings of *moʻo*. A comparative analysis reveals that whatever their linguistic origins, these denotations have come together in Hawaiian culture in this way. They are all concerned with continuity and relationality.

Our moʻo are brindled, another meaning of *moʻo*, which refers to skin or fur with a pattern of darker stripes against a lighter background. Likewise, the darkish uppermost portion of a mountain range (moʻo) stands out against the lighter sky; the uppermost part of a canoe, the gunwale (moʻo), stands out against the ocean; the narrow path (moʻo) stands out against vegetation; as do the raised surface between irrigation areas such as walkways (moʻo) between wet taro patches. Similarly, *moʻo* also refers to that which is part of a larger whole or series, such as a grandchild or great-grandchild (moʻo), or offspring of an animal (moʻo); a smaller piece of bark cloth (moʻo) that will be joined to a larger piece; and a smaller land division (moʻo) within a larger land division. Moreover, Hawaiian reptilian water deities are also termed moʻo. They symbolize continuity because they personify the life-giving and death-dealing characteristics of water, without which life would be impossible. Lastly, *moʻo* is short for *moʻolelo* (series of words or speech), which comprises English genres such as history, legend, and narrative. Moʻolelo impart important lessons, preserve cultural knowledge, and reflect a distinctly ʻŌiwi approach to narration. Unlike the linear narrative approach typical of Western cultures, ʻŌiwi approaches to narration are anything but. I term our narrative strategy "mohala ka pua lehua" (the lehua bud blossoms) where each stamen (narrative elements such as character, place, action) unfurls as the lehua bud (moʻolelo begins) matures (moʻolelo progresses) and fully blossoms (the moʻolelo concludes).

The Past before Us: Moʻokūʻauhau as Methodology celebrates ʻŌiwi brilliance and the continuity of our traditions inspired by such concepts and practices as moʻo, moʻokūʻauhau, and moʻolelo, while commemorating the physical-intellectual-spiritual umbilical cord that unites us with our ʻŌiwi ancestors and Polynesian forebears whence we ultimately originate. We descend from a deeply philosophical people who valued excellence in whatever we did. E ola mau ka poʻe ʻŌiwi a poʻe hoahānau ma Moananuiākea, ko kākou one hānau—long live the ʻŌiwi and our sibling-cousins in the Great-ocean-expanse, our ancestral home-birthplace.

Marie Alohalani Brown

Editor's Preface

Moʻokūʻauhau as methodology is as much about our connections and relationships to places and the natural world, as it is about our past, present, and future people. This understanding is ancestral and intergenerational. In my own lived experience, I gained depth in this practice while sailing with the canoe *Hōkūleʻa* throughout the Marquesas Islands to Pitcairn Island and Mangareva in the Tuamotu Islands, and from Rapa Nui (Easter Island) to Tahiti at the turn of the millennium. While sailing, and upon returning to Molokaʻi, my worldview shifted and I could see and feel the guidance of my ancestors embodied in the natural world.

It was on the Voyage to Rapa Nui with *Hōkūleʻa* that I could clearly make the connection between the relationships that we were developing with the ocean, stars, sun, moon, rain, clouds, wind, with all and everything. One night while on watch, looking at the full radiant moon, its power and wisdom overcame me and I was moved to tears. A vision came into my mind of Kalamaʻula, Molokaʻi, and my grandmother's Hawaiian homestead. This definitive moment altered my direction. Now I see, feel, and interpret the embodiment of our ancestors frequently, no matter where I am in the world. Following this direction is *kūpuna consciousness* or *moʻokūʻauhau as methodology*, extending from our long lineage of understanding and knowing.

Each of the contributors to this collection conceived, explored, and articulated their own knowing of moʻokūʻauhau as methodology, making the chapters diverse and unique. The book developed across many lands and over several years. Our collaboration came together in different hemispheres, islands, and lands. From idea to reality, during the creation of the book, our ʻohana moved from Te Wai Pounamu (the South Island of New Zealand) to the prairies of Edmonton, Canada. It was at the University of Alberta, along the shores of the Saskatchewan River, as a Postdoctoral Fellow that I decided to gather Kānaka from around the globe to create *The Past before Us: Moʻokūʻauhau as Methodology*. During the creation of this edited collection our family made two transnational moves across the world, bringing us to where we now reside in Kirikiriroa, Aotearoa (Hamilton, New Zealand).

The contributors to the book might not realize how central they have been to my sense of direction and purpose over the past few years. I have felt incredibly humbled by the opportunity to facilitate and edit this collection. Our connections expand from being Kanaka ʻŌiwi to global citizenship that crosses and defies imposed boundaries and definitions. We come to represent inclusivity, acceptance, and unity. We explore the core cultural value of moʻokūʻauhau in different ways, while celebrating both our commonalities and our unique approaches. May we strive toward unity and utility in all that we do! This is for all that has come before, our kūpuna, their presence, and for our children, and the next generation of Kanaka ʻŌiwi.

Acknowledgments

Mahalo e nā akua, nā kūpuna, nā ʻaumākua. From the depths of my being, I truly believe that all who have come before guided this work. I acknowledge that the idea for *The Past before Us: Moʻokūʻauhau as Methodology* was a collaborative call, whispered in the wind. When my mind, heart, and spirit were open and still, I listened. I acknowledge our ancestors and their ever present guidance embodied in all and everything. Mahalo nui loa.

Mahalo e nā wahi pana. So many sacred places influenced and shaped our understandings from all over the world, in Hawaiʻi, Minnesota, New York, Canada, and New Zealand. Personally, I acknowledge Kaʻaʻawa, Hakipuʻu, and Palolo on Oʻahu Island; Kalamaʻula and Wailua on Molokaʻi Island; Kaʻū and Kalapana on Hawaiʻi Island; Colorado, Minnesota, Jasper, and Edmonton; Ōtepoti, Kirikiriroa, and Maketū. Mahalo nui loa.

Mahalo Kālepa Baybayan, Bruce Blakenfield, and Nainoa Thompson for welcoming me on the Voyage to Rapa Nui, as well as a special mahalo to my cousin, Manuwai Peters, and Penny Martin who welcomed me home from the voyage and facilitated my knowing in Kalamaʻula, Molokaʻi. Mahalo nō.

Mahalo e ka ʻohana puke, Manulani Aluli Meyer, Kū Kahakalau, Mehana Blaich Vaughan, Kalei Nuʻuhiwa, David Chang, ʻUmi Perkins, kuʻualoha hoʻomanawanui, Lisa Kahaleole Hall, Marie Alohalani Brown, and Hōkūlani Aikau. Mahalo for your patience and perseverence! There are so many people who have been a part of this journey of creation. To those I have not mentioned by name please accept my gratitude. To Noelani Goodyear-Kāʻopua, you were absolutely central to the core participants. I acknowledge you as the force that brought forth such a diversity of contributors, and it is your mana that I believe unifies the collection. No laila, mahalo nui loa!

My gratitude to the Faculty of Native Studies at the University of Alberta for your welcoming community of beautiful people and the office space that you shared during my Postdoctoral Fellowship. Thank you to Professor Brent Swallow, Associate Professor Brenda Parlee, and the Faculty of Agricultural, Life and Environmental Science for your administrative support.

Mahalo nui, ngā mihi to Professor Linda Tuhiwai Smith and Associate Professor Leonie Pihama for welcoming me to the University of Waikato and for the opportunity to work as a Research Fellow at Te Kotahi Research Institute. Ngā mihi nui to our team at Te Kotahi: Leonie Pihama, Papahuia Dickson, Tammy Tauroa, Herearoha Skipper, Te Uranga Paki, Jenny Lee-Morgan, and Joeliee Seed-Pihama for your support in the preparation of this publication. Ngā mihi also to Paulette Bruns and the Waikato Society of Arts for your feedback, support, and use of the studio to paint the cover art.

Mahalo e kuʻu ʻohana. To my parents: Carolyn Louise Averill, I love you and thank you for always believing in me and encouraging me! To my dad, Herbert Ralph Mahie Wilson, mahalo for teaching me through your actions to sit quietly and to listen to the wind, water, rocks, and earth, to the messages of our ancestors embodied all around us. You are an inspiration. Our moʻokūʻauhau is what creates and shapes this journey of learning. Thank you for reminding me that nā kūpuna are always with us. Mahalo nui loa. Aloha nō.

Ngā mihi ki taku hoa rangatira, kuʻu ipo, Brendan James Hokowhitu, aloha wau iā ʻoe, thank you for your attentive listening, patience, and continuous support. Ngā mihi to our big, strong men Tari Jay and Riley, thank you for your hugs and love. Ngā mihi to our babies, Kalikookalani Louise and Tai Kaʻaukai, mahalo nui loa, may the wisdom from these pages guide and inspire you as the next generation of Kamakahukionālani, Honoapiʻilani, Kanakaʻaukai, Kealaikahiki, and the long lineage of our moʻokūʻauhau. Eō!

THE PAST BEFORE US

INTRODUCTION

I Ka Wā Mamua, The Past before Us

NĀLANI WILSON-HOKOWHITU AND
MANULANI ALULI MEYER

"I ka wā mamua," meaning the time in front, is the inspiration for the title, *The Past before Us: Moʻokūʻauhau as Methodology*. "The past before us" in this context utilizes the English language to communicate a Kanaka ʻŌiwi (Native Hawaiian) worldview layered with multiple meanings. It acknowledges all that has come before ourselves, extending beyond the human realm to include the earth, sky, ocean, riverways, plants, animals, stars, moon, and creation in its entirety. I ka wā mamua, stretches all the way back to pō (night/darkness) and ao (the emergence of light) that begin the epic Kumulipo, a creation chant detailing evolutionary biology in 2,108 lines that "establishes moʻokūʻauhau as a foundation of ʻŌiwi culture, identity, and worldview" (hoʻomanawanui 2014, 6). The title does more than honor the past, it reveals its purpose while also acknowledging Kanaka ʻŌiwi ancestors and geneaologies. I ka wā mamua and "the past before us" are utilized to emphasize a vital shift in worldview from "genealogy" as it is understood in English, which prioritizes human kinship relationships, to encompass the vastness of Kanaka ʻŌiwi familial relationships that extend well beyond the human realm to include islands, oceans, planets, and the universe.

Moʻokūʻauhau is fundamental to Hawaiian epistemology and to our sense of knowing and being (Kameʻeleihiwa 1992). In the context of this collection, moʻokūʻauhau is the grounding force that weaves together and synthesizes the chapters. Translation of the term moʻokūʻauhau from ka ʻōlelo Hawaiʻi (the Hawaiian language) to English is mistakenly oversimplified as "genealogy." The depth of moʻokūʻauhau is profound because within the Kanaka ʻŌiwi worldview genealogies extend to the first single-cell organisms.

Moʻokūʻauhau as methodology draws upon the deeper layers of literal, kaona (multiple), and noa huna (secret) meanings in the word moʻokūʻauhau. Moʻo in this context can be defined as a succession, a series, stories, traditions, or lineage. Kū refers to standing upright, stopping, halting, or anchoring, and in another manifestation presides over aspects of battle and warfare. ʻAuhau is the femur and humerus bones of the human skeleton. When strung together moʻokūʻauhau speaks of the succession of our ancestors and the mana within their bones, buried in the ʻāina (land), which establishes our place to stand tall, our place from which to speak, protect, defend, and love. Our moʻokūʻauhau gives us our strength, direction, guidance, and mana.

This collection of Hawaiian scholarship is bound together by a shared and intersecting moʻokūʻauhau (geneaological lineage). All contributors are Kanaka ʻŌiwi, moʻokūʻauhau to Ka Pae ʻĀina ʻo Hawaiʻi (the Hawaiian archipelago), and share their unique methodological perspectives as Kanaka scholar-practitioners. Native Hawaiian, Kanaka ʻŌiwi, Kanaka Maoli, and Kanaka (Kānaka) are all terms used interchangeably in this book to describe the first peoples who are Indigenous and genealogically connected to Ka Pae ʻĀina ʻo Hawaiʻi.

Contributors conceptualized and wrote their chapters exploring moʻokūʻauhau and its utility within their various research areas. Although authors reside across the globe, extending from the Hawaiian Islands to Aotearoa (New Zealand), and Turtle Island in Utah, Minnesota, and New York, they remain connected by a shared moʻokūʻauhau and passion for cultural scholarship and political integrity. A diverse field of academics from political science, English, Indigenous studies, Pacific Islands studies, Hawaiian studies, environmental science, sociology, history, ethnic studies, education, and women's studies highlights for the reader the purpose of transdisciplinary scholarship. The result of our collaboration is a unique collection—inclusive, open, and far-reaching—that gives voice and resonance to contemporary Kānaka and builds upon the growing body of Indigenous methodological scholarship (Smith 1999; Meyer 2004; Denzin, Lincoln, and Smith 2008; Wilson 2009; Kovach 2010; Chilisa 2011; Wilson-Hokowhitu 2012; Andersen and Walters 2013; Oliveira and Wright 2016). Ka wā mamua, the time we face, the things we know, the values we are inspired by, and the wisdom of experience, inform and direct our futures as Indigenous, Pacific, and Kanaka ʻŌiwi.

Native peoples from around the world are experiencing a time of reconciliation, self-determination, healing, and recovery as a result of colonization and the activism of Indigenous peoples to understand and transform cultural and epistemic trauma. It is a process of re-discovery through the revival of culture, history, language, and the responsibility to place. What remains consistent is continuity, moʻo/succession. This is "where the moʻo lives." Moʻokūʻauhau (family continuity) extends a long lineage of strength from the earliest beginnings to the time of our ancestors initial voyages across the wide ocean expanse, mapping stars and sensing tides, over thousands of years establishing relationships with our islands and oceanscapes.

Indigenous peoples are moving beyond a colonizing mentality to join the growing voices that assert our unique epistemologies, survivance, and futurities. Inside us our beloved kūpuna live. Nā kūpuna in the Hawaiian language acknowledges both our elders and ancestors of past and present, living, as well as those who have passed and are embodied in the natural world.

The Past before Us: Moʻokūʻauhau as Methodology is a collection about enduring Indigenous research methodologies with the capacity to be specific and universal, localized and global, while also remaining meaningful. This is the nature of Indigenous thinking, where false dualities are detailed because wholeness is the point of continuity. The collection comprises scholar-practitioners, devoted to reverence, seeking empowering forms of research praxis so that the time we face, will once again be recognizable. In this way, knowledge is deepened and extended.

Where the Moʻo Lives

> Ua ʻikea i ka mauli ola.
> All is known through the source of spirit.
>
> *Pūlama Collier*

Moʻo is both our tangible and intangible forms of expression that affirm consciousness, the root idea of moʻokūʻauhau. Thus, retooling ancestral knowledge for modern relevance is now the practice of continuity. How then do we organize stories, publishing, and ways of researching within an intracultural acumen that articulates, expresses, and extends life? How do we make this world a space to awaken to meaning and begin to care for our lands, oceans, and waterways once again? How do we step beyond predictable academic polemics into the wholeness of life found in the *reverence* of aloha? How do we combine enduring knowledge systems to heal ourselves and connect with those who wish to collaborate? *The Past before Us: Moʻokūʻauhau as Methodology* works to fulfill this spiritual mandate to transform consciousness in ways only island peoples can and must.

These authors come from a lineage of courage, which cultivates both clarity and consciousness. Indigenous knowing does not need to shout, repeat itself, or doubt. It needs only to be clear. This kind of clarity is not typical, mundane, or ego sustaining. It comes from a different geography and set of priorities. It does not work to maintain false dualities because it seeks, instead, to understand and recognize the highest capacity in people. We must focus on prioritizing knowledge based on forms of currency/spirit that work to heal, and that have enlightened principles at the core of their knowing. Here are the ideas that produce continuity.

The Past before Us: Moʻokūʻauhau as Methodology is meant to capture the *function* of Indigenous, Pacific, and Kanaka ʻŌiwi scholarship and to be a vehicle for expanding consciousness. We rise with the full range and depth of our Oceanic clarity expressible here in print form. We respond more deeply to our issues because we are nourished with island epistemologies and friendships that instruct our knowing, our capacity to wānana—to discuss with courage and thus intentionalize our collective futures. Cultural empiricism then can work its magic to reconstruct a society devoted to enduring ideas that make sense from a Kanaka ʻŌiwi viewpoint. History will then have the function to teach us more about continuity. Here is where the moʻo lives.

Hoʻoulu Lāhui o Moananuiākea!

> Puʻupuʻu lei pali i ka ʻāʻī.
> Even the different and imperfect lei is beautiful when worn, like the foliage in the cliffs.
>
> *Mary Kawena Pukui (1983, 303)*

Diversity is essential to the acceptance of oneself and of others. It is the fiber of culture. We have gathered together from across the globe to create a book that focuses on Hawaiian epistemologies and research methodologies. We are simply adding more voices to this growing body of literature available from and by Kanaka ʻŌiwi scholar-practitioners. Our hui represents the potential for lāhui (nation) to extend beyond the shores of Hawaiʻi nei because unity is vital for our future and helps manifest the moʻo of continuity to influence our world in powerful ways. In doing so, we promote awareness and practice the diversity of enduring knowledges and island worldviews. This discipline is fueled by our knowing that aloha is our true intelligence. It is a force that has the capacity to heal our world and propel us into a more sustainable future. Within the pages of this anthology we explore our direct connection to earth, ocean, sky, and people. Our moʻokūʻauhau expresses our deep ancestral relationships to ʻāina and moana. This is the wisdom in *The Past before Us: Moʻokūʻauhau as Methodology* that we seek to share.

The opening chapter, "Māʻawe Pono: Treading on the Trail of Honor and Responsibility," by Kū Kahakalau, presents the epistemological foundations of Māʻawe Pono, which are deeply rooted in the Hawaiian worldview known as kū-a-kanaka. This way of being Hawaiian, and perpetuating Hawaiian language, culture, and traditions in the twenty-first century, grounds both the practical, as well as the theoretical aspects of Māʻawe Pono. The chapter shares the development of Māʻawe Pono and the process of evolution from a mixed methodology to a unique, original methodology. The chapter then presents some of the foundational aspects of Māʻawe Pono that are existentially different from existing qualitative and quantitative methods of research. The chapter ends with a detailed explanation of the eight phases of Māʻawe Pono that constitute its research design. The philosophical premise and distinguishing features of Māʻawe Pono inspire other Pacific and Indigenous researchers to embark on a similar quest to make a social impact and to be empowered to allow research methodologies aligned with their worldviews to evolve and awaken into consciousness.

In "He Haka Aloha: Research as Lei Making," Mehana Blaich Vaughan weaves together teachings and memories of her grandmother. In this chapter, she describes her tūtū, Amelia Ana Kaʻōpua Bailey's approach to making lei wili (wrapped lei) in ten steps. Each step offers lessons for approaching research to learn about a place or ʻāina. Her tūtū was a teacher, offering lei workshops to preschool kids, garden club members, parent volunteers, women in prison, strangers who turned up at her home—anyone who wanted to learn. Vaughan offers these steps as if teaching students of lei making, environmental science, or any exploration of the relationships between people and the places that sustain them. She relates how her tūtū never stopped learning, experimenting, and innovating. She taught a simple technique, while she encouraged each student to be creative, to make it their own. The chapter encourages readers to pick the most useful lessons to make their own, and add beauty to their research, in a way that honors the lessons of their own homes and kūpuna (ancestors).

"Papakū Makawalu: A Methodology and Pedagogy of Understanding the Hawaiian Universe," by Kalei Nuʻuhiwa, discusses how Papakū Makawalu comes from the cosmogonic chant called the Kumulipo, several genealogies compiled into a single composition. Papakū Makawalu is a foundational methodology that systematically organizes the accumulated knowledge obtained through generations of observations and interactions with the natural world. All knowledge and understanding of the surrounding environment were categorized into three distinct houses of erudition: Papahulihonua, Papahulilani, and Papanuihānaumoku. Papahulihonua includes all of the natural earth phenomena and cycles; Papahulilani includes all of the natural atmospheric phenomena and cycles; and Papanuihānaumoku includes all of the living organisms, the affiliated practices, and the social relationships established through the necessity to survive. As an analytical methodology, Papakū Makawalu affords the researcher the ability to thoroughly investigate any subject or topic of Hawaiian epistemologies from multiple perspectives.

Next is kuʻualoha hoʻomanawanui's chapter, "E Hoʻi i ka Piko (Returning to the Center): Theorizing Moʻokūʻauhau as Methodology in an Indigenous Literary Context." The chapter explores how moʻokūʻauhau is an integral cultural concept that underpins Kanaka Maoli society, community, and culture, past and present. As such, it is adaptable to other culturally derived applications aside from just recounting one's personal ancestry. This chapter examines moʻokūʻauhau as a methodology relevant to the study of literature as part of the wider and growing field of Pacific and Indigenous studies. The blossoming of Indigenous studies over the past two decades has prompted calls for the increased articulation and application of relevant, culturally based theories and methodologies across scholarly disciplines. While the chapter focuses specifically on the discipline of literary studies, it is an approach that can be applied to other academic disciplines. Hoʻomanawanui argues that Indigenous, culturally located and derived methodologies such as moʻokūʻauhau are long-standing analytical and intellectual tools that have been used for countless generations within the context of Indigenous education and intellectual traditions; rather than being novel creations, they have been re-discovered, recognized, and utilized by new generations of Indigenous scholars.

"Moʻokūʻauhau and Mana," by ʻUmi Perkins, suggests a way of exploring Hawaiian, Nietzschean, and Foucauldian genealogical methods. Hawaiian genealogies emphasize continuity of ancestral or other lineages, while Nietzschean and Foucauldian genealogies highlight ruptures. By focusing on mana, or power (status, spiritual force), this chapter brings these distinct methodologies into closer resonance. Hawaiian sources demonstrate a surprising comfort with ambiguous and plural origins, a stance that Nietzsche aspired to for European theory. Perkins' research focuses on ʻāina. As ʻāina is viewed by Hawaiians as kin rather than real estate, and land is linked to power, this method functions to destabilize received narratives of land in Hawaiʻi. The chapter proposes a "layered" methodology that is explanatory and comparative, emancipative and deconstructive.

"From Malihini to Hoaʻāina: Reconnecting People, Places, and Practices," by Hōkūlani K. Aikau talks about Aikau's experiences returning to Hawaiʻi nei, after a period of separation, to document the social and ecological impact of the restoration of loʻi kalo (wetland terraced taro fields). She agreed to join the research team because of the opportunity for doing community participatory research in partnership with Kākoʻo ʻŌiwi, and was eager to be part of a process of making the ʻāina momona (abundant) once again. What became immediately apparent when she was introduced to the larger community was that she was a malihini (a stranger) to the place and community.

The chapter examines the "multiple layers of belonging" that she encountered doing community participatory research with an ʻŌiwi community for which she is a malihini. As a Kanaka ʻŌiwi scholar whose moʻokūʻauhau does not connect to the ahupuaʻa of Heʻeia, she questions "the multiplicity of obligations, responsibilities, and audiences" for which she must be accountable. Although she begins with a critical self-reflection of being malihini, she concludes with some reflections on the broader implications of malihini haole (non-Hawaiian strangers) playing a key role in the restoration of ʻŌiwi land-based practices intended to feed the lāhui.

"Transcending Settler Colonial Boundaries with Moʻokūʻauhau: Genealogy as Transgressive Methodology," by David A. Chang, expresses a perspective from the Hawaiian diaspora, exploring how Hawaiian practices of moʻokūʻauhau demonstrate the ways that genealogy can enrich studies of Indigenous peoples, settler colonialism, transnationalism, gender, and sexuality in Hawaiʻi and in other Indigenous contexts. In this chapter, we see how moʻokūʻauhau can permit a deeper historical understanding of the ways racial, national, and colonial boundaries were imposed on Kānaka and the ways Kānaka eluded those boundaries by sustaining alternative geographies of connection. Moreover, Chang concludes that moʻokūʻauhau rightly brings gender and sexuality to the center of the study of these processes.

"All Our Relations: Moʻokūʻauhau and Moʻolelo," by Lisa Kahaleole Hall, reflects on the relationship between moʻokūʻauhau, moʻolelo (story), and kuleana (responsibility/ authority) from the perspective of a multiracial Kanaka Maoli woman who grew up on U.S. military bases. The chapter explores the stories we tell about our relationships. In Hawaiian metaphorical terms, she considers how we face forward toward the past. Neither the past nor the future is linear; we gain knowledge of our roots to shape our present and our futures. Since moʻokūʻauhau and moʻolelo are fundamentally intertwined, this chapter asks what our responsibility is to the knowledges and relationships that form us.

The concluding chapter, "Moʻokūʻauhau as Methodology: Sailing into the Future, Guided by the Past," by Nālani Wilson-Hokowhitu engages moʻokūʻauhau as guidance, drawing upon personal stories from the canoe *Hōkūleʻa*, and global citizenship. The chapter engages moʻokūʻauhau as methodology in multiple ways by interweaving four core values of ʻapo (acceptance), hoʻololi (transformation), hoʻonui (expansion), and lōkahi (unity). At the heart of the chapter is a call for acceptance and openness.

Bibliography

Andersen, Chris, and Maggie Walter. 2013. *Indigenous Statistics: A Qualitative Research Methodology*. Walnut Creek: Left Coast Press.

Chilisa, Bagele. *Indigenous Research Methodologies*. Thosand Oaks: Sage.

Collier, Pulama. 2012. Personal communication. November 8.

Devzin, Norman, Yvonna S. Lincoln, and Linda Tuhiwai Smith. 2008. *Handbook of Critical Indigenous Methodologies*. Thousand Oaks: Sage.

Hoʻomanawanui, Kuʻualoha. 2014. *Voices of Fire—Reweaving the Literary Lei of Pele and Hiʻiaka*. Minneapolis: University of Minnesota Press.

Kameʻeleihiwa, Lilikala. 1992. *Native Land and Foreign Desires: Pehea lā e pono ai?* Honolulu: Bishop Museum Press.

Kovach, Margaret. 2009. *Indigenous Methodologies: Characteristics, Conversations, and Contexts*. Toronto: University of Toronto Press.

Meyer, Manulani Aluli. 2004. *Hoʻoulu: Our Time of Becoming: Early Collected Writings of Manulani Aluli Meyer*. Honolulu: ʻAi Pōhaku Press.

Oliveira, Katrina-Ann, and Erin Wright. 2016. *Kanaka ʻŌiwi Methodologies-Moʻolelo and Metaphor*. Honolulu: University of Hawaiʻi Press.

Pukui, Mary Kawena. 1983. *ʻŌlelo Noʻeau: Hawaiian Proverbs and Poetical Sayings*. Honoulu: Bishop Museum Press.

Smith, Linda. 1999. *Decolonising Methodologies: Research and Indigenous Peoples*. Dunedin: University of Otago Press/Zed Books.

Wilson, Shawn. 2009. *Research Is Ceremony*. Winnipeg: Fernwood.

Wilson-Hokowhitu, Nālani. 2012. "He pukoa kani ʻāina: Kanaka Maoli Approaches to Moʻokūʻauhau as Methodology." *AlterNative, An International Journal of Indigenous Peoples* 8, no. 2:137–147.

1

MĀ'AWE PONO

Treading on the Trail of Honor and Responsibility

KŪ KAHAKALAU

Mā'awe Pono is a Hawaiian research methodology that emerged gradually over the past three decades, awakened into consciousness through intense, heuristic contemplation, extensive, in-depth, informal study, and meticulous, rigorous action research spearheaded by the Kū-A-Kanaka Indigenous Research Institute, involving thousands of Native Hawaiian co-researchers. The term "mā'awe pono" was carefully chosen, after months of prayer, reflection, and ceremony. Hawaiians believe that words have a powerful ability to influence and impact outcomes, as expressed in the proverb, "*I ka 'ōlelo nō ke ola, i ka 'ōlelo nō ka make.* Life indeed is in words; death indeed is in words" (Pukui 1983, 129).

Mā'awe in Hawaiian refers to a narrow path or trail. Pono is everything that is good and right from a Hawaiian perspective. The term "mā'awe pono" according to Hawaiian scholar Mary Kawena Pukui refers to the (right) track of honor and responsibility (Pukui, Haertig, and Lee 1972, 19). This name was chosen for several reasons. For one, just like the ancient trails constructed from smooth river rocks enabled our ancestors to move across miles and miles of rough *'a'a* lava terrain, so does Mā'awe Pono aim to provide a path for Hawaiian researchers to find solutions to current obstacles and issues, restore justice, and bring about *pono* (righteousness).

Moreover, all involved in the research process must purposefully choose to walk the narrow trail of honor and responsibility to ensure that all aspects of the research journey are ethical, or pono, and congruent with Hawaiian cultural values and beliefs. Indeed, Mā'awe Pono holds both the primary researcher, as well as all of the co-researchers, to the highest ethical standards. Specifically, Mā'awe Pono encourages all involved in the research to walk in the footsteps of our ancestors and follow their teachings to the point where Hawaiian values and practices permeate all aspects of the research process. This type of research can be defined as mo'okū'auhau (genealogy) as methodology, since it implies the honoring of the past, which Hawaiians call ka wā imua, or the time before us.

This chapter begins with an exploration of the philosophical and ethical foundations of Mā'awe Pono, deeply rooted in a traditional Hawaiian worldview. This view is reflected in hundreds of Hawaiian proverbs ('ōlelo no'eau), which inform both the theoretical, as well as the practical aspects of Mā'awe Pono. This chapter introduces the methods that make Mā'awe Pono unique and provides a detailed explication of the eight phases of Mā'awe Pono that constitute the research design, and ends with a brief overview of the evolution of Mā'awe Pono, and the process of morphing from a mixed methodology into a distinctly Hawaiian research method. The hope is that it will inspire the next generations of Indigenous researchers, in Hawai'i and beyond, to create new, culturally driven research methodologies, aligned with Native worldviews and designed to advance Native people, protect our land, and perpetuate our languages and cultures.

Ethical Foundations

Mā'awe Pono constitutes research for Hawaiians, by Hawaiians, using Hawaiian ways to advance things Hawaiian and to protect and perpetuate Hawaiian assets and resources, including Hawaiian land, culture, and language. Fortunately, as the motto of Kū-A-Kanaka states, "When Hawaiians thrive, everyone benefits!" While the research is Hawaiian-focused, the outcomes are anticipated to benefit all of Hawai'i. As a Hawaiian research methodology Mā'awe Pono is aligned with the philosophy of kū-a-kanaka, which can be translated as "to stand as a Hawaiian," or "to be Hawaiian." This means that our research is reflective of and aligned with the actions, attitudes, and lifestyles of those who identify as Hawaiian and purposefully, actively, and openly perpetuate the traditions and values of our Hawaiian ancestors in this modern age. While this population is quite diverse, basic tenets shared include participating in Hawaiian arts and sports, speaking the language, practicing Hawaiian protocol, eating from the land and the sea, and striving toward an independent Hawaiʻi.

Māʻawe Pono flows from and is rooted in this Hawaiian knowledge base of kū-a-kanaka, grounded in hundreds of Hawaiian ʻōlelo noʻeau. These proverbs contain clear messages regarding the approach and the purpose of research, and of life. Until the last generation of mānaleo, or Native speakers of Hawaiian, passed away a few decades ago, the use of proverbs permeated Hawaiian conversations. Today we are fortunate to be able to consult *ʻŌlelo Noʻeau: Hawaiian Proverbs and Poetical Sayings* (Pukui 1983), an invaluable resource of almost three thousand Hawaiian proverbs, representing the collective wisdom of our ancestors, their dreams and aspirations, their values, standards, and non-negotiables. These proverbs, which are saturated with metaphorical language, convey our ancestral virtues and attitudes and constitute our behavioral guidelines, by telling us how to think, how to talk, and how to act. Māʻawe Pono advocates that as twenty-first-century Hawaiian researchers it is our responsibility, or kuleana, to know our ancient proverbs and use them in daily conversations. We must also practice what they teach and apply the insights provided by these proverbs to our daily lives. Māʻawe Pono also promotes using our Hawaiian proverbs as concrete guides to navigate the research process. By integrating the very poetic, very direct, and exceptionally witty and funny messages of our ancestors into our research we also assure that our methodology is and remains Hawaiian.

Māʻawe Pono uses Hawaiian proverbs as guidelines for various aspects of the research process, starting with our general attitude about learning and seeking knowledge, which is captured in the proverb, "*He lawaiʻa no ke kai pāpaʻu, he pōkole ke aho; he lawaiʻa no ke kai hohonu, he loa ke aho*. A fisherman of the shallow sea uses only a short line; a fisherman of the deep sea has a long line. A person whose knowledge is shallow does not have much, but he whose knowledge is great, does" (Pukui 1983, 80). This proverb admonishes us to learn all we can about our Native ways and advance them into the future. It also asserts that as researchers we must become well acquainted with the phenomenon to be researched. In addition, the proverb reminds us that engaging in research increases our connection to the deep sea of knowledge of our ancestors.

Māʻawe Pono's commitment to take things to the highest level, grounded in the Hawaiian proverb, *Kūlia i ka nuʻu*, which means "strive to the summit," has been a standard for Hawaiians for many generations. In fact, this quest for excellence has resulted in widely recognized Hawaiian expertise in areas as diverse as voyaging, horticulture, functional arts, leʻaleʻa (gaiety), extreme sports, green technology, natural resource management, and island sustainability. For twenty-first-century Hawaiians, this ancient mandate to excel continues to fuel our work, including our research, as we strive to return to food sovereignty, economic sustainability, community-based resource stewardship, political independence, normalization of the Hawaiian language and Hawaiian cultural practices, and individual and collective happiness. The determination to implement positive change, no matter how large the problem, is in line with the teachings of our ancestors expressed in the proverb: *"ʻAʻohe puʻu kiʻekiʻe ke hoʻāʻo ʻia e piʻi.* No cliff is so tall that it cannot be scaled. No problem is too great when one tries hard to solve it" (Pukui 1983, 25).

Māʻawe Pono is also aligned with the Hawaiian philosophy of *makawalu,* which literally means eight eyes. The meaning of makawalu is explained in the proverb, *"Peʻapeʻa maka walu.* Eight-eyed Peʻapeʻa. One who is wide awake and very observant; one who is skilled. Peʻapeʻa was the son of Kamehamehanui of Maui" (Pukui 1983, 288). Māʻawe Pono fosters this propensity to be wide awake, very observant and skilled, and poised to see everything with eight eyes, or from multiple perspectives. This multidimensional perspective makes Māʻawe Pono exceptionally flexible and fluid. It allows for the seamless ebb and flow from the past to the present to the future and back again. Another aspect of makawalu is the fact that it at once localizes and globalizes our knowledge base. While Māʻawe Pono has first and foremost a local, Hawaiʻi-based focus, it also provides a viable tool to investigate some of the unique issues that affect Hawaiians on the continent and abroad. This population continues to grow, as a result of an increasing number of Hawaiians suffering economic hardship in our homeland.

Distinguishing Qualities

As a distinctive twenty-first-century Indigenous research method, Māʻawe Pono incorporates a number of special qualities not necessarily unique or exclusively Indigenous, but that collectively distinguish Māʻawe Pono from other methodologies. These qualities include the relations and roles of the various participants in the research process, the purpose of the research, the methods employed, and the impact made.

One distinguishing quality of Māʻawe Pono is the intense involvement of the primary researcher in the research process, a feature shared with many other Indigenous methodologies. This involvement begins with the question, or the phenomenon, to be researched, which has to matter personally to the primary researcher. Data suggests that when the question is aligned with the researcher's personal ʻiʻini, or desire, there is generally a passionate, disciplined commitment to remain with the question intensely and continuously until it is illuminated, or answered, regardless of the time involved. Māʻawe Pono asserts that as the researcher allows passion, compassion, and comprehension to mingle, the unity of intellect, emotion, and spirit, known as lōkahi, becomes transparent.

The intimate personal involvement of the researcher is in contrast to colonial, academic models, which support a separation between the researcher and the research project. These positivist research methodologies purport a "rigorous scientific methodology applied by a rational, neutral, and objective subject to the study of an object clearly positioned outside of himself" (Strega 2015, 122). This means that the researcher is expected to remain neutral and unbiased, removing his/her personal opinion from the research process. For Hawaiians, this notion of neutrality is incomprehensible, because Hawaiians believe that we bring our *mana*, or personal power, to every situation and every task. This includes all our strengths: physical, emotional, intellectual, and spiritual. It also includes our knowledge, skills, and experiences, our hopes, dreams, and visions, as well as our ancestral endowments, like our moʻokūʻauhau, or genealogy, and the wisdom shared by our ancestors while we sleep. These cumulative experiences influence what we do as children, grandchildren, siblings, spouses, parents, grandparents, and friends. They also influence our behavior as researchers. In fact, it is this personal mana, or spiritual power, contributed by the researchers to the research process, that gives Māʻawe Pono the power to be a change agent, a beacon of hope for Indigenous communities to solve our own problems.

Māʻawe Pono believes that the best way to gain expertise in any subject is to become intricately involved in the phenomenon. This participatory role of the researcher is grounded in the proverb, "*Nānā ka maka, hana ka lima.* Observe with the eyes; work with the hands. Just watching isn't enough. Pitch in and help" (Pukui 1983, 247). This ancient statement validates that just observing from afar is of little value. Moreover, once the eyes observe, there is a responsibility to act by imitating what was observed or by using the information gained through observation to achieve the goal. Māʻawe Pono suggests that as the primary researcher personally encounters and interacts with the phenomenon, remaining open, receptive, and attuned to all facets of the experience, knowledge is discovered. This knowledge gradually continues to grow as a result of the researcher's direct experiences throughout the research process, explicated through multiple processes, senses, and sources. Since the primary researcher is expected to become an expert on the research topic, it is essential that all who use Māʻawe Pono as a research methodology come with a solid background in things Hawaiian, including our language, cultural values, and practices. Such researchers must also know Hawaiian protocol, history, and prominent issues facing modern Hawaiians and our archipelago.

Another distinguishing aspect of Māʻawe Pono concerns the concept of time. Māʻawe Pono aligns with existing heuristic practices, which require the researcher to take the time to allow things to evolve, and revelations to formulate. In fact, one of the eight phases of Māʻawe Pono specifically allots time for indwelling and reflection, requiring the primary researcher to become receptive and to listen to her na'au (gut), regardless of how long this process will take. This inherent mana of patience, well known by our elders, is expressed in the saying, "*E ho'omanawanui*. Be patient" (Pukui and Elbert 1983, 238). This popular saying reminds researchers to take time to reflect and allow ancestral 'ike (knowledge) and recent insight to interact and surface as new knowledge. Furthermore, rather than operating according to a calendar that focuses on the completion of deadlines, Mā'awe Pono advocates for an organic accomplishment of the task at hand, regardless of the length of time involved. Finally, contrary to heuristic methods, which are designed to study past and present phenomena, Mā'awe Pono is timeless in that it can also be used to explore phenomena, which are currently evolving, as well as those still to be born in the future.

As a participatory method of research, Mā'awe Pono requires the active involvement of a specific group or community concerned with the issue at hand, who become essential co-researchers in the process. In fact, rather than postulating the primary researcher as an authority figure who collects, interprets, and presents the findings, Mā'awe Pono situates various groups of co-researchers as joint contributors and investigators. By leveraging insider knowledge, collaborators assure that the research actually addresses their needs and that solutions are found. This process also validates the experiences of the participants, assists in the development of critical skills, and elevates community members to expert status. Moreover, by becoming collaborators, rather than merely subjects, the co-researchers play a crucial role, not just in the gathering, but more importantly in the interpretation, of the data.

In order to assure a successful collaboration it is essential that the primary researcher has cultivated strong personal relationships with the community, and the various research participants. This is essential, because, contrary to most Western research projects, where the researcher and participants have a time-limited relationship that expires when the project is complete, Indigenous research in and for Native communities builds on long-term, familial relations between the researcher and the participants. Data shows that personal relations with the primary researcher motivate co-researchers to stay with the project and finish what was started. Moreover, engaging collectively in a worthwhile project has shown to result not only in personal satisfaction, but also in collective efficacy.

As a Hawaiian methodology, Mā'awe Pono advocates and uses methods of data collection, analysis, and presentation that are culturally congruent. These culturally based methods align with Hawaiian values and have been used by our ancestors for thousands of years. They are valid simply because they have withstood the test of time. Interestingly, most of these Hawaiian methods align with methods of data collection, analysis, and presentation used by Indigenous scholars elsewhere.

One important method used by Māʻawe Pono to gather data involves observation, substantiated by the proverb, *"I ka nānā nō a ʻike*. By observing one learns" (Pukui 1983, 129). This proverb clearly validates observation as a successful Hawaiian method of collecting data used by our ancestors. *"Nei ka honua, he ʻōlaʻi ia*. When the earth trembles, it is an earthquake. We know what it is by what it does" (Pukui 1983, 251). This is another proverb that legitimizes observation. In fact, the use of observation as a research method dates back thousands of years, when our ancestors in central Polynesia used their observations of the patterns of migratory birds, and other phenomena, to hypothesize that there were islands to the north. This theory prompted them to set out on a journey over thousands of miles of open ocean until they discovered the Hawaiian archipelago about two thousand years ago.

The concept of intense, keen observation of a phenomenon or problem, often over long periods of time, and by multiple experts, is an essential component of Māʻawe Pono. One of our most well-known Hawaiian proverbs states, *"Nānā ka maka, hoʻolohe ka pepeiao, paʻa ka waha*. Observe with the eyes; listen with the ears; shut the mouth. Thus one learns" (Pukui 1983, 248). Our ancestors even created a proverb to describe a careful observer, calling him, *"Ka manu kaʻupu hālō ʻale o ka moana*. The kaʻupu, the bird that observes the ocean" (Pukui 1983, 160). This propensity of being keen observers of our surroundings is a trademark recognized easily among Hawaiians even today. In fact, this predisposition to continuously observe one's environment provided our kūpuna a solid knowledge of their place, as is reflected in the following proverb, *"ʻŌlelo ke kupa o ka ʻāina ua mālie, ua au koaʻe*. The natives of the land declare the weather is calm when the tropic bird travels afar" (Pukui, 1983, 273). This proverb substantiates the reliability of data gained by observation and confirms that the findings of those intricately involved in the research are valid, especially when patterns clearly replicate themselves.

Another culturally congruent aspect of Māʻawe Pono is the fact that the primary researcher and the various teams of co-researchers know, adhere to, and practice Hawaiian protocol at all times. Hawaiian protocol can be defined as doing the right thing, at the right time, for the right reason. From a Hawaiian perspective then, practicing Hawaiian protocol is part of our effort to create and maintain a state of pono, or righteousness. Practicing Hawaiian protocol in research is necessary to assure that the interactions between people, the environment, and the spiritual world are pono (appropriate) at all times. This means that before starting any task relating to the research, the researcher(s) must connect with the spiritual world. It also means that we continuously acknowledge our ancestors and the role of spiritual guides in the research process and ask for their blessings and support as we complete the various phases of the research.

Practicing Hawaiian protocol also implies that we follow Hawaiian rules of engagement when interacting with others, including asking permission to enter someone's house, removing our footwear when entering, bringing gifts, honi (kissing) the people involved in the research, and assuring that the heads of younger persons remain below the head of older people at all times. These rules also mandate that the researchers conduct appropriate entry and exit protocol when interacting with the natural world and that there is no damage to people or the environment as a direct, or indirect, result of the research.

Māʻawe Pono also involves finding informants who have a strong background in the issue to be solved. Seeking the input of those close to a situation or problem is a well-known Hawaiian practice, described in the following proverb: "ʻO ka uhiwai nō kā i ʻike i ka ʻino o ka wai. Only the mist knows the storm that caused the streams to swell—only those who are close to a person/situation know the problem(s)" (Pukui 1983, 266). However, rather than using formal structured interviews to gather data from these sources of knowledge, Māʻawe Pono relies primarily on more informal, conversational methods, what Hawaiians call "talk story." This generally involves informants and co-researchers sitting together and informally discussing the research question, or aspects of the research question, in a safe, familial environment. It is this atmosphere of aloha, or love and compassion, that allows the researchers as well as the informants to share their knowledge and expertise in an open, nonthreatening way.

In cases where there are large groups of co-researchers or informants, and/or where there is a hierarchical relationship between the researcher and the co-researcher(s) and/or informant(s), Māʻawe Pono advocates the integration of technology as a nonconfrontational method, which cleverly addresses the issue of "face." This issue is an important factor within Indigenous communities, since there is generally a tendency to avoid conflict, especially with elders and cultural or academic experts. As a result, rather than telling how they really feel, Indigenous co-researchers and informants tend to keep both their praise and their criticism at a minimum, since it is considered impolite and embarrassing to praise or to criticize others. One way to eliminate this issue of "face" is by using email interviews, which are generally viewed as indirect responses to a computer question, rather than a direct response to a specific, known researcher. Research over the past three decades shows that these e-interviews work especially well soliciting honest opinions from Native high school and college students, who are generally very comfortable with technology. Other uses of technology, which make Māʻawe Pono cutting edge, include the use of tools like SurveyMonkey and Facebook to gather data, and Zoom video conferencing to hold focus group discussions.

One traditional Hawaiian way of problem solving has always included experimenting or testing the phenomenon at hand. This could be as simple as throwing a ti leaf into a pool of water to test if a moʻo (dragon) or other supernatural creature is lurking in the water. If the ti leaf floats the water is safe for swimming. If it sinks, the deity is home and the water is not safe. Our medical kāhuna (experts) also used experimentation and tests for diagnosis and prognosis. In fact, when unsure of a procedure or practice, a proverb suggests, "*E hoʻāʻo nō i pau kuhihewa.* Try it and rid yourself of illusion" (Pukui 1983, 35). In other words, try the matter out and the guessing, whether it works or not, is over. This type of experimentation, generally known as action research, is also aligned with the proverb, "*Ma ka hana ka ʻike.* By doing one learns," which purports that Hawaiians establish facts and principles from experience and deduce theory from practice (Pukui 1983, 227).

Action research is by design collaborative, emphasizing community participation, requiring participants to have some level of investment in the study and share a desire to bring about meaningful social change at a local level. In fact, "the values embedded in the action research process are expressed in a discourse of 'sensitivity,' 'respect,' 'self empowerment,' professionalism,' 'collaboration' and 'shared responsibility'" (Somekh 2006, 47). Māʻawe Pono has purposefully been designed to be action-oriented, and make a difference in Hawaiian communities. Centuries of practice confirm that collective commitment, fortitude, and courage allow us to tackle even gargantuan problems and achieve success beyond our wildest dreams. This process of pooling our strengths with others to find solutions to the issues facing our land and our people is called kūkulu kumuhana in Hawaiian. Māʻawe Pono relies heavily on this concept of collaboration, articulated in multiple Hawaiian proverbs, including the following call to come together to tackle a given task: "*E ala! E alu! E kuilima!* Up! Together! Join hands!" and "*Pūpūkahi i holomua.* Unite in order to progress" (Pukui 1983, 32). By incorporating collective inquiry and experimentation Māʻawe Pono wants to assure that Native communities are active participants in charting their future.

Indeed, Māʻawe Pono carries with it a clear directive to initiate social impact and bring about visible, measurable progress toward a goal. This aim is supported by the Hawaiian proverb, "*He ʻike ʻana ʻia i ka pono.* It is recognizing the right thing. One has seen the right thing to do and has done it" (Pukui 1983, 98). Linda Tuhiwai Smith writes that research that involves Native people, as individuals or as communities, should set out to make a positive difference for the one researched (Smith 1999, 131). Māʻawe Pono is dedicated to the betterment of Hawaiian people and our environment by solving problems either specific to a Hawaiian community, or something affecting most, or even all, Hawaiians. Interestingly, most phenomena that matter to Hawaiians, often also have larger social, and perhaps universal, significance. Therefore, although the context presented in this chapter is clearly localized, there is infinite potential for much larger, even global impact, in line with the motto: think globally, act locally. So while Māʻawe Pono is clearly a kanaka (Hawaiian) methodology, the concepts presented can also be useful, not just for other Indigenous peoples, but for a non-Indigenous, global audience.

The Eight Phases of Mā'awe Pono

Mā'awe Pono is made up of eight phases designed to follow one another in consecutive order. These phases, which can differ significantly in length, are designed to guide the primary researcher and the various groups of co-researchers through the research process. As with all aspects of Mā'awe Pono, each of the eight phases is grounded in the wisdom of our Hawaiian ancestors as expressed in our proverbs. While the primary researcher is involved in and responsible for all eight phases, the co-researchers and the community are primarily engaged during the second, third, seventh, and eighth phases of the research.

The eight phases of Mā'awe Pono include:

1. **'Imi Na'auao**—Search for Wisdom
2. **Ho'oliuliu**—Preparation of Project
3. **Hailona**—Pilot Testing through Action Research Project
4. **Ho'olu'u**—Immersion
5. **Ho'omōhala**—Incubation
6. **Ha'iloa'a**—Articulation of Solution(s)
7. **Hō'ike**—Demonstration of Knowledge
8. **Kūkulu Kumuhana**—Pooling of Strengths

PHASE 1: 'IMI NA'AUAO

The first phase of Mā'awe Pono takes its name from the traditional Hawaiian way of discovery and problem solving, called 'imi na'auao, which literally means "to seek wisdom," or "seeking an enlightened gut." The directive to 'imi na'auao and find enlightenment and initiate positive changes has been passed down to us in various proverbs including, "*Lawe i ka ma'alea a kū'ono'ono. Take wisdom and make it deep*" (Pukui 1983, 211).

During the 'Imi Na'auao phase the primary researcher conducts a preliminary assessment, which begins with identifying an obvious issue in the community that is aligned with personal interests and passions. This issue must be relevant and real. The identified need is then carefully analyzed and narrowed down or focused according to severity, urgency, community buy-in, and timing. Acting when the opportunity presents itself is a very Hawaiian way, since we always want to assure the community that the task is performed under optimal conditions. This preference is captured in, "*E kanu i ka huli 'oi hā'ule ka ua. Plant the taro stalk while there is rain. Do your work when opportunity affords*" (Pukui 1983, 39). In other words, if the researcher perceives that it is not a good time to pursue a specific research topic, Māʻawe Pono suggests that she select another. Once the phenomenon has been narrowed down, a specific research goal and research question are formulated that will directly impact the researcher's community. This is followed by an informal inquiry assessing the rationale, practicality, and feasibility of the study. The *'Imi Naʻauao* phase concludes when the researcher determines that the problem is relevant and that there are sufficient resources to conduct the research and solve the problem.

PHASE 2: HOʻOLIULIU

The Hoʻoliuliu phase is known as the preparation phase, where the researcher explores what is already known about the phenomenon, brainstorms possible solutions with various stakeholders, and begins to develop a clear plan of action to tackle the problem. This phase also includes mapping out the research design, strategies, and components, and identifying the specific resources needed to execute the research plan. Our ancestors placed a high value on being prepared, as the following proverb verifies: "*ʻAʻohe ʻulu e loaʻa i ka pōkole o ka lou*. No breadfruit can be reached when the picking stick is too short" (Pukui 1983, 25). This proverb reminds us that there is no success without preparation. During the Hoʻoliuliu phase, the researcher prepares for the process ahead by visualizing the big picture that will be affected by the research, determining both the large scale and long-lasting impacts, as well as the direct and immediate benefits. However, instead of merely developing a hypothesis, the researcher develops an actual solution with a concrete plan of action. This solution is tested via a short-term action research project, which is planned and designed during the Hoʻoliuliu phase.

The Hoʻoliuliu phase is also the time for the primary researcher to select the various co-researchers and identify the roles of both. Another vital aspect of this phase is establishing and/or solidifying personal relations between the primary researcher, the various co-researchers, and the impacted community. Making time and effort to establish amicable, familial relations among all research participants is crucial, because a lack of trust can tremendously limit the outcome of the research. Indeed cultivating strong, trusting relationships between the primary researcher, co-researchers, and the community is vital in achieving success.

PHASE 3: HAILONA

The third phase of Māʻawe Pono, called Hailona, which means "to test," refers to an actual testing of the hypothesis through short-term action research. During this phase, the primary researcher is responsible for setting up and implementing an authentic, community-based action research project involving multiple co-researchers. This action research project should be designed to test a potential answer to the identified problem using a trial-and-error method strategy. Specifically, the action research project should test the general validity of the hypothesis on a small scale by gathering and analyzing quantitative and/or qualitative data using culturally congruent methods. The data can range from quantitative data like statistics or survey data, to qualitative data like salient threads from discussion groups, information gathered through talk-story sessions with experts, or standardized, open-ended e-interviews involving various co-researchers. In addition to providing data to answer the research question, the action research project should also have some immediate positive impact and initiate some measurable positive outcomes for a specific community. At the same time, the lessons learned should be expandable and be able to address the needs of Hawaiʻi's Native people and/or our land as a whole.

PHASE 4: HOʻOLUʻU

The Hoʻoluʻu phase is a time for the primary researcher to immerse and submerge herself in the phenomenon practically day and night, to the point where pretty much everything in life becomes crystallized around the question. During this phase, the researcher looks at and analyzes all of the data gathered in the Hailona phase, searching for common themes and salient threads. If necessary, this is also the time to seek additional, external input from elders and/or experts, or via a review of additional literature, in an effort to gain more understanding of the phenomenon.

It is during this phase that the researcher begins to live the question in waking, sleeping, and dream states. Learning in and from dreams is a way of gathering data highly valued by our ancestors. In fact, a common question, posed by Hawaiian language speakers was, "*He aha ka puana o ka moe?* What is the answer to the dream? What will the result of this be? (Pukui 1983, 61). The value of dream learning has always been understood by Hawaiians as a resource to tap into insights hidden deep within us, as the following proverb indicates: "*Ka pō nui hoʻolakolako, ke ao nui hoʻohemahema.* The great night that provides, the great day that neglects. The gods supply, but man does not always accept with appreciation. Guidance is given in dreams that man often misunderstands and neglects" (Pukui 1983. 166).

During the Hoʻoluʻu phase the researcher spends countless hours in self-reflection and self-dialogue in quiet periods. Clark Moustakas believes that by engaging in ongoing self-searching and self-discovery, the researcher creates an environment that allows the research question and the methodology to flow from inner awareness, meaning, and inspiration (1990, 11). As the researcher contemplates the phenomenon, she allows specific notions to awaken into consciousness from deep within the naʻau. Naʻau in Hawaiian literally means gut. It is that which connects us with the tacit ʻike (knowledge base) of our ancestors. This *naʻau*, when calibrated correctly according to the standards of our ancestors, becomes a powerful gauge to measure what is pono, or righteous, and what is not. In fact, using our *naʻau* to find solutions has always been a very Hawaiian technique. The Hoʻoluʻu phase comes to an end when the researcher, after intense and extensive contemplation and deliberation, formulates a conclusion.

PHASE 5: *HOʻOMŌHALA*

The Hoʻomōhala phase is a period of incubation, where the researcher temporarily steps away from the issue. During this period, the researcher retreats from the intense, concentrated focus on the question and allows the inner workings of the tacit knowledge and intuition to continue to clarify and extend understanding on levels outside immediate awareness (Moustakas 1990, 29). This concept has also been used by great thinkers like Paulo Freire. After finishing *Pedagogy of the Oppressed*, a project he had immersed himself in day and night, Freire was advised by a friend to lock away his work and "let it 'marinate' for three months, four months, in a drawer" (Freire 1994, 48). When re-reading it a few months later, Freire discovered that his book needed one more chapter in order to be complete. During this phase, the primary researcher avoids all conscious thinking or conversation about the research question or any of the solutions. As the researcher distances herself from the phenomenon, allowing the knowledge and insights accumulated through various aspects of the research to marinate for a while, organic, unconscious growth and development occur, intuitions surface, discoveries and illuminations happen, awakened out of obscurity and the supernatural darkness, called pō (night), which is the realm of the gods.

Indeed, the researcher has reached the final stage of the Hoʻomōhala phase when insights awaken into consciousness that may have always existed and are certainly logical. Yet it took extensive reflection and inner growth for these revelations to become apparent enough to be articulated in words. Depending on multiple variables, arriving at this point may happen relatively quickly, or it may take many years for illumination to occur.

PHASE 6: HAʻILOAʻA

The sixth phase of Māʻawe Pono is called Haʻiloaʻa, which literally means, "say what has been gotten." This phase encourages the researcher to undertake a thorough analysis of the various data, insights, and revelations accumulated during the previous phases and articulate her findings. Specifically, this phase triangulates the data procured as part of the research, and officially synthesizes the various aspects of the project. If necessary, this phase also allows the researcher to re-examine areas that are not yet clearly understood. In the end, the Haʻiloaʻa phase should produce a clearly articulated solution to the problem, based on insights gained by the researcher as a result of the research. In addition, the Haʻiloaʻa phase should finalize a viable action plan with short-term and long-term impacts, designed to bring about the desired results.

PHASE 7: HŌʻIKE

The seventh phase of the Māʻawe Pono process is called the Hōʻike, which means "to exhibit," where the primary researcher and her team present the cumulative findings of the research to one or more authentic audiences. Hōʻike is a traditional Hawaiian form of assessment that has been used by our ancestors since the beginning of time. This performance-based assessment can take numerous forms and involve multiple audiences. For example, it can consist of a simple, oral and/or audiovisual presentation of the outcome of the research and the solution to the problem. Or, it can be a creative synthesis of the research presented to the community with whom the research was conducted in diverse forms, ranging from a story map to a hula (dance) drama. In addition, the researcher may also prepare other theoretical or creative contributions to scholarship to external audiences, including academia, funders, and planners. While such sharing is important, Māʻawe Pono purports that the affected community must always be the first and foremost audience to be informed about the research outcomes in a form that is understandable to that community.

PHASE 8: KŪKULU KUMUHANA

The final phase of Māʻawe Pono is called Kūkulu Kumuhana, which means the pooling of strengths for a common purpose. The Kūkulu Kumuhana phase focuses specifically on growing the bigger picture and creating a comprehensive depiction of the core or dominant themes that drive our quest for systemic change. During this phase, which is usually absent in Western research paradigms, the primary researcher actively seeks approval and buy-in from the community in question, to implement the solution(s) presented in the research Hōʻike. Once this implementation takes place, the current research cycle has officially ended and a new research cycle is about to start, which is a typical phenomenon of participatory action research. Moreover, as each cycle is a scale-up from the previous action research project, there is ongoing growth as solutions are implemented, their impact measured, and new answers pursued.

As an Indigenous research methodology Māʻawe Pono is designed to provide answers to pertinent questions and solve specific problems, making a real difference in Hawaiian communities, preferably both short term and long term. Such impact can only be achieved when the research is organized and well arranged, following a specific plan, with specific rules and assumptions based on long-standing premises. Māʻawe Ponoʻs eight-phase process constitutes such a plan.

Challenges and Limitations

The ongoing lack of systemic support for community-based, culturally driven endeavors of any kind, including Native research and problem-solving efforts, severely limits the practice and use of Māʻawe Pono to solve the many problems facing Hawaiian communities. This lack of systemic support results in a general lack of resources, including research funding to use Māʻawe Pono or other Indigenous research methods to test hypotheses and/or implement solutions for Hawaiʻi. Therefore, although we are frequently able to identify solutions to initiate positive change, the fact that there is little or no systemic support and/or resources seriously limits the success of our research. This is the reason Indigenous scholars believe that if research is to play "a useful and progressive role in the process of decolonization, it will ultimately require a political commitment in support of Indigenous peoples and an unambiguous recognition of the colonial role played by mainstream paradigms" (Menzies 2001, 33). Māʻawe Pono asserts that in addition to political support, successful Hawaiian research also requires ongoing access to funding to execute the research. This funding should especially be provided by those who have benefited from Hawaiian resources from colonization to the present, which includes the federal, state, and county governments.

Other limitations involve clashes between traditional values and modern realities. For example, the traditional focus on excellence and the completion of a task, regardless of the time involved, impacts the use of Māʻawe Pono as a research methodology for Indigenous graduate students within Western academia, as well as Indigenous researchers working on grants and other time-sensitive research projects. In other words, the timelines and time restrictions imposed on the researcher by outside entities like universities, grantors, and others, frequently make it very hard for Indigenous researchers to employ methodologies like Māʻawe Pono. This is because these methods often involve longitudinal research and a long-term commitment on the part of the primary researcher to stay with the project, sometimes for years and even decades, since many issues facing Hawaiian communities today cannot be solved even over several years.

Another challenge involves establishing and maintaining collaborative relations between multiple groups of community co-researchers. These co-researchers range from individuals with extensive academic backgrounds and research experience, to co-researchers with strong cultural connections and inherent Hawaiian problem-solving practices. Getting these groups to collaborate is one of the main challenges of the primary researcher who must assure that those with extensive cultural backgrounds and connections to

ancestral knowledge are not made to feel inferior, and those whose creden-
tials are validated by academia are not criticized for being unable to think
and act in a Hawaiian context. Balancing these attitudes and opinions can
be an arduous task for the primary researcher who must also make sure that
no one uses the research as an opportunity to advance themselves and their
agendas. Such egoists can seriously jeopardize any research project because
they do not really want to solve the problem at hand.

THE EVOLUTION OF A METHODOLOGY

When I first began to explore research methodologies for my doctoral research in 1996, there was very little information about Indigenous research,
or anything else Indigenous for that matter. In fact, before I could officially
begin my doctoral work in Indigenous Education, I had to present a paper to my committee and the dean of the university, qualifying Indigenous
Education as a field of study. In the absence of Indigenous research models,
I began to explore existing Western methodologies in the hope of finding a
methodology aligned as close as possible with my worldview, which I could
utilize for my research. While quantitative methods failed to resonate with
my objectives and goals, the then emerging field of qualitative research,
specifically empirical phenomenological research appeared promising. This
qualitative design focuses on the wholeness of experience, rather than solely
on objects or parts, and searches for meanings, rather than measurements.
Other existing Western research methodologies that naturally aligned with
my worldview included exploratory research and observation and participatory action research, which have been used by our Hawaiian ancestors for
thousands of years. In some way, all of these Western experience-based ways
of learning, discovery, and research aligned closely with what is known in
academia as "heuristics," an approach to research that employs a practical
method to reach an immediate goal. Non-academics frequently simplify this
technique by referring to it as using the rule of thumb, making an educated
guess, or relying on intuitive judgment. Yet, both heuristics, as well as the
logical, commonsense approaches to research of my Hawaiian ancestors,
use a rigorous process, following a multiphase journey, which empowers
the researcher to thoroughly interact and bond with the phenomenon being
studied to awaken a solution that could only evolve through experience and
practice, by having "a direct, personal encounter with the phenomenon being
investigated" (Moustakas 1990, 14). Another thing that attracted me to heuristics was the fact that it not only allowed, but necessitated, the researcher
to formulate questions and problems reflecting the interest, involvement, and
personal commitment of the researcher.

Along with exploring existing Western methods, I also began to attempt
to identify specific Hawaiian methods of data collection and presentation,

and the various roles of the researcher, co-researchers, and the Hawaiian community in the research process. Much of this investigation involved the study of Hawaiian proverbs. This research led to the creation of a method I called Indigenous Heuristic Action Research, which I described as a mixed methodology after reading *Decolonizing Methodologies: Research and Indigenous Peoples*, by Linda Tuhiwai Smith. Smith asserts that most Indigenous methodologies are a mix of existing methodological approaches and Indigenous practices. Smith believes that this mix reflects the training of Indigenous researchers, which continues to be within the academy, and the parameters and commonsense understanding of research, which govern how Indigenous communities and researchers define their activities (1999, 143).

In retrospect identifying Indigenous Heuristic Action Research as a mixed methodology was valid, since I used it to meet Western university requirements, and because most tenets of this method were based on existing Western ways of research. Since then I have continued to experience ongoing growth and insight as a Hawaiian researcher specifically, and a Hawaiian cultural practitioner, in general. This growth has led me to realize that the methodology that eventually evolved is actually a new and unique research method, distinctly different from existing methodologies and thoroughly Hawaiian. This notion is in alignment with Wilson's notion that Indigenous methodologies are rooted in Indigenous philosophical positioning or epistemology. Wilson (2001) argues that it is not the method that is the determining characteristic of Indigenous methodologies, but rather the interplay, or relationship, between the method and paradigm and the extent to which the method is congruent with an Indigenous worldview.

Although initially a mixed methodology, over the past decade, *Māʻawe Pono* has evolved into an authentic Hawaiian method of research, demonstrating and validating that Indigenous peoples can and should conduct quality scholarly research utilizing innovative ways of inquiry that align with Indigenous worldviews. This notion continues to grow not only among Indigenous researchers, but also in academia, where acceptance of Indigenous paradigms is on the rise, although Kovach is correct in stating that the nuances and complexities that define Indigenous paradigms may still not be fully understood, or viewed as legitimate, by all members of the academy. At the same time, according to Kovach, academics today would not openly contest, at least in public spaces, that an Indigenous paradigm exists (2009).

Māʻawe Pono opens the door for Indigenous researchers around the world to create and utilize methodologies that are inherently Indigenous and have a standard of complexity and sophistication, equal in scope and breadth to established Western ways of research. This quest for Indigenous researchers to design their own Indigenous methodologies is also reflected in the mission of the American Indigenous Research Association founded in 2013, which is to educate researchers and the public about the importance of

Indigenous Research Methodologies and to promote incorporation of these methodologies into all research that engages Indigenous peoples and communities. Such research should take place not just at institutions controlled by Indigenous peoples, or in disciplines oriented toward Native Studies, but also at the most conservative and prestigious Western universities and in fields seemingly unrelated to Native life and Native ways.

Conclusion

Māʻawe Pono constitutes my effort to decolonize methodology within my own cultural context as a Hawaiian and participate in research on my terms. These terms are defined by the practices of my Hawaiian ancestors and congruent with my Hawaiian moʻokūʻauhau and worldview grounded in the Hawaiian doctrine of kū-a-kanaka (stand as a Hawaiian). Māʻawe Pono is my way of asserting my right as an Indigenous researcher and scholar to design and utilize a way of research that reflects and aligns with a Hawaiian framework and Hawaiian paradigms. Our ancestors clearly realized that as Hawaiians, our ways to approach things are different from those of foreigners that we call haole. This is reflected in the proverb, "*Haole kī kōlea.* Plover shooting *haole*. Blundering foreigner. The haole, in going plover hunting, shoots with his shotgun, killing some, maiming others. The maimed can fly elsewhere to die or become victims of some other animal. But the Hawaiian goes quietly at night with a net. He takes what he wants and lets the others escape unharmed" (Pukui 1983, 57).

These fundamental differences between Western and Hawaiian mindsets also exist when it comes to research, validating the need for Hawaiian research methodologies. Māʻawe Pono articulates such a methodology that is clearly Hawaiian, grounded in the incredible wisdom and knowledge of my Hawaiian ancestors. When King Liholiho, son of Kamehameha the Great, visited England in 1824, he was complimented by the people of London for his intelligence and level of education. To this King Liholiho replied: "*Na wai hoʻi ka ʻole o ke akamai, he alahele i maʻa i ka hele ʻia e oʻu mau mākua.* Who would not be wise on a path walked upon by my parents and ancestors?" (Pukui 1983, 251). As Indigenous researchers, we must honor the past before us with confidence in our traditional ways and reliance on the teachings of our ancestors as we take our rightful place as contributing members of the international community of researchers, on our terms.

Bibliography

Freire, Paulo. 1994. *Pedagogy of Hope: Reliving* Pedagogy of the Oppressed. New York: The Continuum Publishing Company.

Kovach, Margaret. 2009. *Indigenous Methodologies: Characteristics, Conversations, and Contexts.* Toronto: University of Toronto Press.

Menzies, C. R. 2001. "Reflections on Research with, for, and among Indigenous Peoples." *Canadian Journal of Native Education: Sharing Aboriginal Knowledge and Aboriginal Ways of Knowing* 25, no. 1:33.

Moustakas, Clark. 1990. *Heuristic Research: Design, Methodology, and Applications.* Newbury Park: Sage.

Pukui, Mary. 1983. *'Ōlelo No'eau: Hawaiian Proverbs and Poetical Sayings.* Honolulu: Bishop Museum Press.

Pukui, Mary, and S. H. Elbert. 1971. *Hawaiian Dictionary.* Honolulu: University Press of Hawaii.

Pukui, Mary, M. D. Haertig, and E. W. Lee. 1972. *Nānā I Ke Kumu (Look to the Source),* vol. II. Honolulu: Hui Hānai.

Smith, Linda Tuhiwai. 1999. *Decolonizing Methodologies: Research and Indigenous People.* London: Zed Books.

Somekh, Bridget. 2006. *Action Research: A Methodology For Change and Development.* Maidenhead: Open University Press.

Strega, Susan. 2015. *Research as Resistance.* Toronto: Canadian Scholars Press.

Wilson, Shawn. 2008. *Research Is Ceremony: Indigenous Research Methods.* Manitoba: Fernwood.

2

HE HAKU ALOHA

Research as Lei Making

MEHANA BLAICH VAUGHAN

E lei kau e lei hoʻoilo i ke aloha.
Love is worn like a lei in all seasons, Love is everlasting.

> *Pukui,* ʻŌlelo Noʻeau: Hawaiian Proverbs and Poetical Sayings

My research focuses on ʻāina, land, or that which feeds. There is no ʻāina without people, those who are fed by a particular place. I work to illuminate relationships between people and particular places in Hawaiʻi. How do people learn about and use particular places? How do these places sustain families and communities? In turn, how are these communities working to care for the places that sustain them? How are responsibilities to ʻāina being learned and taught to future generations?

I learned to pay particular attention to ʻāina, with an eye for what lei could be made from each place, from my grandmother, my tūtū, Amelia Ana Kaʻōpua Bailey, a lei maker. Tūtū was self-taught or, as she liked to say, "a renaissance lei maker." She meant that she was swept up in the re-emergence of Hawaiian lei as part of the resurgence of our culture in the 1970s. She was not fortunate enough to be taught by her kūpuna (elders), but learned through trial, error, and simply falling in love with the art.

Tūtū always loved lei. Her oldest child, my mom, remembers wearing poepoe (sewed round) plumeria lei to school over her handmade muʻumuʻu (a Hawaiian dress) on May Day. Tūtū didn't become captivated by traditional Hawaiian lei until Mom and Dad chose to have a Hawaiian wedding. Dad and the groomsmen wore aloha shirts, Mom wore holokū (a long Hawaiian dress with a train), and wanted a lei poʻo (head lei). It was hard to find anyone making head lei in Honolulu in 1968 so Tūtū and a friend from the garden club wired white kukui blossoms together and invented one. Tūtū was hooked. After the wedding she took apart the long, thick green lei mom and her bridesmaids had carried, special ordered from Barbara Meheula on the Big Island, to see how they were made. She started going to Bishop Museum to find pictures of Hawaiians wearing lei. She sought out master Hawaiian lei makers, like Meheula and Marie McDonald, and sat for hours cleaning flowers for them, learning by watching. She took her new interest to work as costume director for theater productions at Punahou School and soon taught all her green room volunteers. They started selling lei at the school's annual carnival, the beginning of the now forty-year-old, still thriving, haku lei booth.

Tūtū made all styles of lei, but her specialties were puakenikeni and lei wili. She grew the pua kenikeni in her yard, and picked each morning, climbing the ladder well into her seventies intent on getting every blossom. Lei wili are made using fiber to wrap flowers tightly together. Though she was fifty by the time she started to make lei, once she had learned, she wanted to share.

Tūtū taught lei making workshops to students of all ages, from preschoolers to kūpuna. She taught workshops in public and private schools, her home, hula hālau (schools of learning), preschools, colleges, and at the Daughters of Hawaii. When Tūtū took part in the Garden Club of Honolulu's lei making outreach efforts at the women's prison in Waimānalo, she dressed in a distinguished blouse and culottes set. When she arrived the guard said, "I'm sorry aunty but you cannot come in here. No shorts allowed." Tūtū thought for a moment then said, "Do you have an extra one of those inmate jumpsuits?" She climbed into the neon orange coveralls, belted them smartly, set her haku (head lei) on straight, and headed in to teach her workshop. Here, I offer lessons for conducting community based research on ʻāina, as if giving a workshop to students, sharing some of Tūtū's lessons for making wrapped, or wili, lei.

ʻĀina Uluwehi: *Every lei is a unique reflection of the ʻāina from which it is made*

When Tūtū rode in a car, she was always looking out the window, her eyes tracing the trees, the bank along the side of the road, even the median strip of the freeway. She was known to pull over and dart across four lanes of traffic to gather salmon-colored bougainvillea. Whether driving the saddle road on Hawai'i Island, a stretch of the North Island of New Zealand on her one trip abroad, or the streets of her own Mānoa valley, she was watching for flowers. Every landscape offered a unique lei to be made. The same native plants grow so differently in different places, that in combination with other flowers, and ferns gathered from the same area, they create a lei that reflects one place alone.

Research can also weave new knowledge of landscapes. My work studies a place and its natural resources through weaving together stories of their use. My tūtū saw not just the flowers, but the lei they could make, and got to know a place by creating from it. Seek to interview people who know the land through living from and with it. Learn about 'āina from how people interact with it, across generations. As one lawai'a (fisherman) once told me, "How will we know the health of the ocean, if we are not eating the fish." If you listen to the stories of many different practitioners, and bring them together, you can weave something different from any one family's story, a lei, that combines materials to help each flower be seen in a new way, creating a larger perspective on the place and community it represents.

Hō'ihi: Give back before you take

When Tūtū took us hiking in the mountains, we picked pala'ā fern along the trail to hili or braid as we walked, then tied these lei around our heads. Then we stopped picking until we had reached our turnaround point, the end of the trail for that day. There, we would leave our fern lei behind, placing them on a tree branch, at the base of an 'ōhi'a tree, or offering them at the overlook. Only on the way back, after gifting these first lei, would we gather other materials, such as more ferns and some liko (leaf buds of 'ōhi'a trees), to take home.

Give back before you take. As students and researchers, there is so much you can give to the communities where you work. You have time, research skills, and ability to access archives and electronic databases, which are expensive, far away, and challenging for community members to use. Imagine if every researcher who worked in a place simply gathered the studies that had already been done on that place for the community. You can pull together everything from EIS documents to historic maps to past oral histories, sources you should compile for your work anyway, that most community members have likely never seen. You can also give back in more immediate ways. Volunteer for community work days and projects, long before you start asking questions, or if possible, even forming them.

Mālama: Take only what you need and take care

Tūtū taught us not to pick too much from any one plant, just a bit here and there. As you gather materials to make lei, move around, trimming to keep plants healthy, go slowly so as not to break a branch. She taught us to cut ferns at the very base of the stem, cleaning the patch as we went, stacking them neatly, taking our time with each frond. Through hālau hula (training in hula), I learned other specific ways to take care of plants my hula sisters and I gathered flowers from. We are taught to go first to weed beds of fern, and to pick off the stem of the maile vine after stripping the leaves so that it does not rot back to the mother plant. We clean our materials in the forest, leaving twigs and leaves we will not use in our lei to mulch the base of the plant we are picking from. At hālau lei making sessions we keep two sets of trash bags. One is to throw away ʻopala (rubbish) such as string or napkins. The other is for discolored leaves, extra stems, and any plant material separated out in the making of lei, which are saved and returned to earth, so that no piece of kino lau (many forms of akua or gods), gets tossed in the trash. Tūtū used everything, teaching us to care for and not waste anything we picked. She painstakingly tended the materials in her flower fridge. She re-soaked ferns and wrapped them in newspaper, saying, "Natives love newspaper." She refilled glass jars of water holding stems, spraying each stalk by hand, checking all of the flowers every day. Her care made the materials she gathered last for weeks. Like Tūtū's flowers, kino lau (the embodiments of gods) fed by sun and nurtured by rain, the stories gathered in your research are sacred. It is your responsibility to harvest gently, to take only what you need, and to care for and use all that you pick.

Kuleana: Harvest first from the place you know and cultivate

As Tūtū got older, she got worried about stresses on the mountain plants in areas where we gathered flowers and ferns for lei. Invasive grasses crowded out fern beds while the leaves on ʻōhiʻa lehua trees started to reveal spots and galls from new pests. So that she didn't have to "take," from the mountains, Tūtū became an avid gardener, cultivating everything from ʻohai aliʻi to bleeding heart, gardenias to green roses, cup and saucer to eucalyptus, to many varieties of liko lehua, all in her own yard. In my favorite photo of Tūtū she is sitting by one of her palapalai fern beds, wearing a purple bandana and waving a Japanese sickle at the camera. Her hands rest on her outstretched knees as she takes a break from cutting dried brown fronds and weeding out grass from her ferns, a task she did a few times each year.

Consider whether you might be able to cultivate a research site in your own hometown, or in a place you have already been working, rather than going to another community. It takes time to get to know a new community, its lands, people, and issues. The jobs you have done leading up to college may not hold the work you aim to do in life. However, the places you have worked, relationships you have built, and past connections to particular landscapes are worth continuing, and may offer key research questions or sites. Like Tūtū, I try to gather flowers first from my own backyard, focusing most of my research efforts in my home community, growing only slowly to extend investigation of the same questions to other places by invitation.

Aloha aku, Aloha mai: Cultivate relationships

Tūtū did not have to tell us not to pick from someone's yard without asking. We never visited strangers' yards asking for flowers because Tūtū had already cultivated so many friendships. If someone had an interesting tree or shrub in their yard, Tūtū made friends with them long before it started to bloom. She had friends all over Mānoa valley, made lei for their children's special occasions, and knew their favorite flavor of homemade jam. Many began planting things in their yard just for Tūtū. In the mornings, she would load us grandchildren, multiple jars of jam, and a long pole clipper in the back of her station wagon and drive around Mānoa, visiting people and picking. One Japanese neighbor spent the afternoon showing us the collection of pōhaku kuʻi ʻai (stone poi pounders) he had both carved and found. The tree outside his house exploded with red lehua—orangey, with wide brushy fibers. We listened and talked story, picking only on the way out. Even when buying flowers, it was about the relationships. Tūtū knew every employee at Watanabe Floral, her favorite flower shop, and all about their families because she always took time to visit.

Interviewing, like gathering flowers to make lei, requires cultivation of relationships. Start with people you know and allow them to introduce you to others. Before you interview someone, particularly elders, make time to take them food, help out in their yard, drive them to the doctor. Always go back multiple times to meet, talk story, get a sense of their stories and interests, and to explain your work. If possible, take them to visit the places they have mentioned. After conducting interviews keep going back to listen to new things people may have remembered, review transcripts for accuracy and comfort, and just to see how people are doing. Whether in the forest, someone's yard, or their garage for an interview, take time, cultivate relationships, ask permission, go slow, and give back before you take.

ʻIke: Every hand makes a different lei

To Tūtū, every lei truly was beautiful. People learning at her workshop would groan that their novice effort was inferior to another student's lei, or to Tūtū's. "Mrs. Bailey, My lei is so fat. So skinny. It is twisting all over the place. It doesn't look anything like yours." Tūtū would reply, "I've been making lei for thirty years. This is your first. You're a natural." She would lomi (massage) the lei a bit, and exclaim, "There you go, lovely!"

Tūtū always reminded students not to try to be like someone else. "Each lei maker is different," she would say, "Only you have your hand." Tūtū's most experienced lei maker friends loved to work together on big jobs because even working from the same gathered materials, they created unique lei of varying widths, weights, textures, and highlights. These expert lei makers loved watching one another work and relished the surprise of seeing the final lei all together. When looking at lei, Tūtū could often identify their maker by some distinguishing detail like how that person used a particular fern.

Similarly, your research will be yours alone. Another student asking the same questions in the same situation might well come up with different answers. This does not mean your answers are not true, but that each person sees and renders the world differently. Natural science research is often suspicious of subjectivity, striving for replicability, where any research team that conducts the same study following the same procedures should get the same results. Let your research, like lei, be shaped by your hands, the changing environment from which you gathered your data, and the guidance of the community in which you work. This subjectivity, your unique perspective, is necessary, unavoidable, and a strength. At the same time, try to gather diverse materials from a range of sources. Talk to people with different points of view and backgrounds, so as not to see things in only one way.

Hōʻakoakoa: Gather a diversity of materials from different sources

Tūtū's lei stood out for the diversity of materials she used. For special projects, like weddings, she started scoping flowers months before. She harvested for a week leading up to big events, visiting multiple friends' yards, trimming bushes around her house, driving back and forth to Watanabe Floral, and picking bougainvillea in the parking lot when she came to pick me up from high school in the afternoon. Tūtū used ten or fourteen different plants in one head lei—leaves, seed pods, berries, green calyxes of lehua whose blossoms had fallen off, rakishly orange ranunculus, and distinguished silver liko. Each lent different heights—spiky and nestled—colors, greens, textures, and a touch of yellow ginger buds for fragrance. These diverse materials set one another off in new light, creating a unique and unexpected whole.

In your research, strive to bring together varied sources of data to create new ways of seeing an issue. In addition to interviews, I draw on meeting observations, community member surveys, policy document analysis, focus groups, moʻolelo (stories) in Hawaiian language newspapers, mapping, ecological data, and lots of time just being in a place. Each source of information compliments others to offer a more complete picture of a place and the community shaped by it. My tūtū relied on her network of friends across Hawaiʻi to drive far from Hilo town to check aʻaliʻi patches, or to send hydrangea from their yards in upcountry Maui. Do not try to gather all data yourself. Rely on colleagues, students, and friends to apply their skills and methods in multiple areas, bringing together increasingly multidisciplinary teams to create new knowledge and ways of seeing.

Proceed one step at a time and let the outcome surprise you

I loved to sit on the cool concrete steps next to Tūtū's lei table watching her work while KCCN Hawaiian radio played over the hum of her flower refrigerator. As hard as I tried, watching her gnarled fingers cluster flowers, the decisive wrap and pull of her raffia, I could never discern a pattern in her lei. Tūtū shook her head at the thought of pattern, of set repetition. When people in lei workshops asked her if there was some order in which they should place flowers into their work, she directed: "Just look at the lei you are making and add what it needs next." Through trial and error, her students quickly gained the sense that red lehua blends in next to crimson aʻaliʻi, but it catches the eye if added after fern and a yellow rose. Slowly, one flower, one fern, one wrap at a time, they learned to see.

Allow yourself to develop a sense of what your lei will look like as you go. Not until I have gathered all of my flowers, prepped, cleaned, sorted, and laid them out on the table, do I have any inkling of the final product. Not until I begin to wrap the materials together, adding each flower at least once, do I see what the lei might become, and not until I'm finished, do I know for sure.

Let your research carry the same sense of unexpectedness. Though you start an interview with a set of questions, you cannot know what the person you are sitting with will talk about. Follow where they lead. Use your interview questions as a map of a landscape, not a step-by-step trail guide. At some point, gather flowers and greenery from each part of the terrain. Cover the map, but not in any set order. Environmental research, like lei making requires trusting the people who know a place, and your own naʻau sense (your gut or intuition), more than any pattern or plan. After finishing your interviews, sort (or code) them. Place all the roses together, then clean them, take off the dead leaves and thorns. Sift through the information in each category and take out what you cannot use. Then begin to weave the rest together.

Tūtū rarely lingered over a finished lei. She simply tied off her raffia, snipped stems, dunked the lei in water, gave it a shake, then tucked it into a towel in her flower fridge. Her favorite was always the last lei she called "kalakoa," using whatever flowers remained on the table. Perhaps she was most surprised by how this lei of leftovers would turn out. Even with all of her experience, lei making held an element of surprise for Tūtū, and well into her eighties she continually tried new ways to seek the unexpected and to learn.

Wili: One technique, many forms

Using her simple three-strand wili method, Tūtū created everything from fat, heavy lei for the necks of horses in pāʻū units of parades, to dainty circlets of baby's breath and roses for the heads of three-year-old flower girls. She made table decorations, pew swags, kāhili (towering standards designating royalty) that stretched from floor to ceiling in four corners of a grand room, sweeping hats made of flowers for Parisian-themed garden shows, boutonnieres for proms and more, all using the same wili wrapping technique. Sometimes people were amazed that she could weave such diverse creations. Tūtū would just laugh and tell them, "You can create all sorts of things that only you can imagine. It just takes a little experimentation and a lot of practice."

Researchers often think of research products in terms of theses, journal articles, or books, mostly catering to other academics. Instead, think of how your research, and the set of methods you use, can yield different products for diverse audiences. Examples include interview transcripts and recordings for an interviewee's family, a short video about the place you are studying, information on species health in particular gathering spots shared only with those practitioners who harvest there, and layered maps portraying how different groups see and use the same place. Research I have worked on has been shared in coffee-table photo books with quotes from interviews, two-page summaries of research findings, poems, and two eulogies for elders I interviewed over many years. You can share your findings in children's books, websites, testimony and policy briefings for government decision-making bodies, along with PowerPoint presentations, journal articles, and other more conventional forms. All of these different products, like lei wili, derive from the same set of methods and body of research. Yet each gives back to the place and community in which you have worked in a different way, sharing learning to build capacity to care for that place.

One place where Tūtū did not experiment was craftsmanship. All of her creations were made by wili, and each was wrapped firm. I remember toiling for hours to make a lei at one of her carnival workshops as a high school freshman. I took a long time and was embarrassed that upperclassmen in charge of organizing the workshop were sweeping up around me by the time I was done. Tūtū came over, picked up the finished lei and, to my horror, began to swing it around over her head vigorously, lasso style. When no flowers dropped, she placed it back on the table saying only, "If a lei is well made, it will not fall apart when you do that." In research too, your arguments will hold up if you create them carefully, with attention and skill. Get to know your methods well, practice and master them so that you can use them to create in never-before-seen ways. Honor the knowledge and tools your teachers have given you and build beyond them. Craft your research carefully, make multiple varied products of quality. You will find that each finds its own right audience, and that your work will be used, loved, and shared.

E Mau: No lei lasts forever, process over product

Lei making is a process that yields lasting learning and joy long after the final product, the lei itself, is gone. People often asked Tūtū to make everlasting lei. Some even offered to buy artificial flowers for her to wili. She always refused, "The beauty of lei is that they are not meant to last forever." Days of gathering and cleaning flowers and ferns, then weaving them together, yield a lei that may last mere hours. However, the memory of its fragrance, the feeling of wearing the lei, the experience of making it, the combination of flowers and scents that will never be replicated exactly, all linger. More important than the lei itself, its fleeting beauty, is the process of making it.

Your research can also yield lasting learning long after the project, thesis, article, or paper is finished, if you think of your work as a process. The research process should build community members' capacity to care for and learn about their own places. Participatory research engages people in designing and carrying out studies of the places they have ancestral ties to, harvest from, and care about. People work together to develop research questions, gather and analyze data, develop answers to the questions they have raised, and act upon those answers, all the more powerfully for having generated them. Wherever possible, employ local students: just out of high school, attending community college, or home for summer from a four-year university. This employment can contribute to both students' desire, and their financial ability to continue their education, while showing how education can lead to a career that allows them to give back at home. Consider your research as a way to not only learn from a place and its community, but to build lasting capacity, relationships, and abilities within the place and people you work with, which will flourish long after you are gone (Vaughan 2015).

Pīpī holo kaʻao: The story goes on

Tūtū not only never went empty-handed, she always went laden. For any event, she'd make a lei for the host and guest of honor, pua kenikeni or haku for her entire table of friends, plus her own lei poʻo (head lei). She even took a lei to the Pro Bowl for Joe Montana, whom she loved. She clambered down the stands to hang over the tunnel when he ran off the field after the game, yelled "Joe," and hurled her lei. When she went to a Nakeʻu (beloved Hawaiian fashion designer) show, or Christmas fair, her offerings of lei filled the car. Tūtū's largesse was fueled by her boundless energy, and hard work. You could never beat Tūtū to a task and it was a rare achievement to finish something before she told you to do it. Even in her seventies no matter how early you got up to help load her car for an event, she'd have been up an hour earlier and done it already. She never procrastinated, always planned ahead, and tackled the hard things first. She was also never idle. If there was a family event with lei kuleana pau, she'd say, give me something to do, and set to work chopping vegetables, juicing citrus, or weeding. For Thanksgiving and any family occasion, she'd always make lei for all our extended family. She simply loved to share.

Lei are meant to be given and shared, so that they may be worn. Lei add beauty and fragrance, which spread from the recipient, throughout the event he or she attends. Research too should not sit in a fridge, journal, or dissertation, but must be shared and distributed, used and shared again. Through sharing, research can make circumstances better, and add to 'ike (knowledge), that which is seen, smelled, sensed, experienced, and known.

Even if Tūtū could not give a lei in person, or made it for someone else to give, people recognized her lei. She took time to wrap each creation in a pū'olo of ti leaves, adorned with a nosegay made of the same materials as the lei, hinting at the beauty inside the package. In your research, develop your own style, apply it well, and present the results of your labor wholeheartedly, with love. Then, teach and share your style with others.

Though Tūtū did not learn to make lei from her kūpuna, she was proud that her seven mo'opuna (grandchildren) can say we did. Tūtū gave me my first basket of lei making supplies at age five. It contained a long needle taped in a cardboard paper towel roll, clippers, raffia fiber, a spray bottle, and clothespins. She taught her sons, daughter, nieces, nephews, hula family, and friends. All over Hawai'i hands of people who took one of hundreds of Tūtū's workshops are making and sharing lei and teaching what they have learned because Tūtū loved and chose to share. You too may find that teaching is the best part of your research, allowing learning to blossom and continue in ways you could never imagine. When a lei is pau and dried beyond wearing, even on a hat, we return it to the 'āina, back into the palapalai (fern) beds in Tūtū's yard or our own, place it to adorn a tree or encircle roots. Like dried lei returned to the 'āina whose seeds sprout into a new 'a'ali'i (*dodonaea viscosa*) bush, teaching is a way of sharing that bedecks the 'āina, abundant and thriving with blossoms for more lei, *mahuahua a manomano a lei*.[1]

People often asked Tūtū her secret to looking so young and happy. She always told them, "I make a lei every day." Water always flows to the sea, evaporates into clouds, and rains on the forest and the lehua trees still blooming in my tūtū's yard in Mānoa. At the end of each lei workshop she taught, Tūtū liked to say, "Today is the first day of your new life. You will never look at the world in the same way again. Everywhere you go you will notice what is growing, in your neighbor's yard, in your own." May your research shape the way you see the world and approach learning about and caring for the places you love, and may it shape your students to plant seeds to grow and bedeck the 'āina a mau loa aku (always).

Notes

For my grandmother, Amelia Ana Ka'ōpua Bailey.

Mahalo to my tūtū (grandmother) and all of the 'ohana (family), as well as the friends, students, and community members who shape my work.

1. These words, meaning growing strong, productive, abundant, thriving, and bedecked, are from the oli Māewa i ka Hao Mai a Ka Makani, written by haku mele (composer) Kainani Kahaunaele. This chant celebrates the growing process of 'a'ali'i, a hearty bush with windblown seeds that flourishes in challenging conditions.

Reference

Vaughan, Mehana. 2015. "*Mo'olelo 'Āina*: Stories of A Place." In *'Āina Based Environmental Research Hawaiinuiakea: Methodologies for Conducting Research in Indigenous Communities*, vol. IV, edited by Kapa Oliveira and Erin Kahunawai Wright. Honolulu: University of Hawai'i Press.

3

PAPAKŪ MAKAWALU

A Methodology and Pedagogy of Understanding the Hawaiian Universe

KALEI NUʻUHIWA

Hanau Laumiha hanau ma ka lolo
O Kahaula wahine hanau ma ka lolo
O Kahakauakoko hanau ma ka lolo
O Haumea o ua wahine la no ia
Noho ia Kanaloaakua
O Kauakahiakua no a ka lolo
Hoololo ka hanauna a ia wahine
Haae wale ka hanauna lolo
O Papahulihonua
O Papahulilani
O Papanuihanaumoku, e ola! (Beckwith 1951, 232)

Papakū Makawalu is a paradigm that comes from the cosmogonic chant called the Kumulipo that systematically organizes the accumulated knowledge obtained through observations and interactions with the natural world and the natural systems over many generations. All knowledge and understanding of the Hawaiian environment was categorized into three distinct houses of learning: Papahulihonua, Papahulilani, and

Papanuihānaumoku. Papahulihonua covers all natural earth phenomena and cycles; Papahulilani covers all natural atmospheric phenomena and cycles; and Papanuihānaumoku covers all organisms, and any practices and relationships necessary for their survival. As an analytical methodology, Papakū Makawalu affords the modern Hawaiian researcher the ability to thoroughly investigate any subject or topic of Hawaiian epistemologies from multiple perspectives. As a pedagogy, Papakū Makawalu provides the educator with a holistic approach to teaching any Hawaiian topic, practice, or phenomenon, which in turn, offers the learner deeper insight into the meaning of the Hawaiian Universe. This chapter explicates the Papakū Makawalu process as methodology and pedagogy by analyzing a section of a genealogical chant from the perspective of each house of knowledge.

Moʻokūʻauhau (Genealogy)

From the Hawaiian perspective, moʻokūʻauhau is generally considered a genealogical map of the origins of all things that are birthed. Moʻokūʻauhau also includes the inception and creation of anything tangible, intangible, animate, inanimate, built, birthed, or created. Simply stated, a moʻokūʻauhau is a recorded explanation of the kumu (origin or source) for anyone or anything that has come into being or into existence. Most Hawaiian stories begin by identifying the kumu of the important characters followed by the subsequent sequenced connections. Generally, the genealogy will continue until it reaches the characters whose stories are being related. This initial identification of a character's kumu and circumstances of existence that follow thereafter serves to validate the truth of a story or history. Providing a moʻokūʻauhau at the onset of any kind of story authenticates the account. Furthermore, this discursive strategy provides listeners with the necessary background information for accessing the narrative and internalizing it. Listeners may discover connections between themselves and the characters, with the story becoming a personal experience for listeners through their genealogical connection to the characters.

The term "lipo" means dark, ancient, primordial, or anything that is indiscernible. A good example of lipo is a forest seen from a distance. You can see that there are many trees of varying shades of green and other dark colors, but you cannot differentiate one tree from the next; yet you know that individual trees exist. For the purposes of this chapter, the term lipo is interpreted as primary or principal. When these two words, kumu (origins) and lipo (primary), are brought together, one interpretation is "Primary Origins."

Kumulipo (Creation Chant)

The Kumulipo was a genealogical creation chant composed for a chief named Kalaninuiʻīamamao (Johnson, vii). The Kumulipo is a compilation of several genealogies amassed into a single composition noted for its moʻokūʻauhau characteristics beginning with the origins of life in the ocean and on land, and the emergence of humans. The Kumulipo also notes the beginning of the recognition and categorization of consciousness, and the emergence of religious and political practices pertinent to the sanctification of a chief. There are several different versions of the Kumulipo. This chapter focuses on a portion of the composition called the Kalākaua Text.

The Kalākaua Text contains sixteen wā or epochs, which are laid out as chapters. The chapters map out the beginning of tracking time followed by the birthing of living organisms. Life begins with the primordial organisms found in slime and quickly progresses to coral, marine life, bird life and winged creatures, to four-legged animals, and finally people. After a lengthy time of the rise and fall of people, families, and political movements, the focus alters, and a new era evolves.

Following a genealogical format, most of the wā in the Kumulipo begin by identifying the male first and then the female partner. In wā thirteen, a notable shift occurs. Females are listed first, followed by their male partner. The thirteenth wā occurs during the time of Haumea. Haumea is the ancestor who was very concerned with the genealogy of her progeny. Notably, she chose women from her lineage to become the leaders and to pursue the systematic exploration of the human consciousness. Haumea's female descendants were also given the title Haumea based on their active leadership role during wā thirteen. In wā thirteen, the Haumea women are born from the brain, which is called puka ma ka lolo. Symbolically, to puka (be born) ma ka lolo (from the brain) would mean that the practitioner was now developing new philosophical thoughts and practices out of a foundational framework, whose name will be shared shortly. Subsequently, the women are credited with intentionally working toward naming and categorizing their surroundings into three distinct groupings. Under the leadership of the women, individuals became responsible for understanding their surroundings, which then led to their becoming experts in the three fields of study. The three distinct categories of knowledge that were created were Papahulihonua, Papahulilani, and Papanuihānaumoku.

The Papa Houses of Knowledge

Pualani Kanakaʻole Kanahele began studying the Kumulipo in the 1970s, a historically important decade that saw the restoration and revitalization of Hawaiian knowledge and practices.[1] Sometime later, she noted the genealogical reversal within the Haumea section and realized that the intellect of experts was being formalized. The realization came to her through the following lines of wā thirteen (line numbers below):

1792. O Papa-huli-honua
1793. O Papa-huli-lani
1794. O Papa-nui-hanau-moku (Beckwith 1951, 232)

Kanahele explained that each word was intended to be a single sentence that deliberately captures the attention.[2] Papanuihānaumoku is widely understood by Hawaiian communities. Papa is the deity connected to the progenerative capabilities of all organisms. Papahānaumoku practitioners are experts tasked to memorize the genealogies of living beings. It became clear to her that the Papahulihonua and Papahulilani were in all probability the same types of experts and practitioners. Kanahele explains:

> Each word or line is a House of Knowledge. Each house of knowledge encompasses one third of their [Hawaiians'] universal knowledge, and together they envelop their universe. . . . These houses of knowledge delineate three classes of Kahuna practitioners. They are experts in their field of knowledge, gnosis and profundity. This is a way of learning a diminutive component while having some perspective of the full extent of the whole. Today we investigate their system of knowledge and specialties to see through their eyes the universe in which they, as well as we, live. (1)

Papahulihonua includes all of the natural earth phenomena and cycles. The experts within this house of knowledge studied the natural divisions, cycles, and activities of the ocean, water, geology, geography, volcanology, and any other earth-related natural process. Papahulilani includes all of the natural atmospheric phenomena and cycles. The experts within this house of knowledge studied the natural cycles, divisions, and activities of the sun, moon, stars, clouds, wind, stratums, climate, and time tracking. Papanuihānaumoku includes all living organisms. The experts within this house of knowledge studied the genealogies of notable individuals, health and well-being–related practices, politics, and the social interrelationships between all living beings established for the necessity of continued survival. Papahulihonua and Papahulilani are based on the cycles and processes of nature void of human interference. Papanuihānaumoku is mainly concerned with the reproduction processes that also include humans and the human impact in the natural environment. All three houses of knowledge can be used to examine a single subject at its most natural kumu from three different perspectives, providing a holistic and comprehensive overview of that single subject.

Experts belonging to each of these three houses of knowledge were responsible for the survival and continuation of pertinent information. Like the Kumulipo and other genealogical chants, information was purposely placed within the poetry and imagery in order to remain available beyond the time of composition. The poetry and imagery within the chants are timeless images of cycles and events that occurred in the past and exist in the present. Chants are the mechanism by which data was stored. Thus, researchers and scholars can access data from the ancestors in the chants that have survived the passage of time.

Following the Kumulipo and the methods recorded in wā thirteen during Haumea's era, Kanahele developed the Papakū Makawalu process based on these three houses of knowledge with the objective of utilizing the large database found in chants to access the information preserved within them. Ua puka ma ka lolo. Puka!

Papakū Makawalu

The term "papakū" can be broken down into two main concepts. The first part, papa, can be translated as a foundation, such as a topic or subject. The second part, kū, can be translated as something that is established, such as a core or nucleus. Therefore, the term papakū can be interpreted as the core entity or main subject. A papakū can be any subject, topic, or entity that is analyzed within the three houses of knowledge.

The term "makawalu" can be translated as multiple perspectives. It also describes tumultuous movement. Makawalu is more of an image of an action, feeling, or experience than a simple word. A good example would be a flowing river. A river is a single body of water in motion; however, when it reaches a descent in the riverbed, it becomes a waterfall. At that point, the river becomes thousands of individual drops of water. Fundamentally, it is still the same river, but individual components of this body of water are now moving out of its original form. That action or movement is the imagery of makawalu. The subject starts out as an established entity or topic whose original body provides the foundation for the many components that emerge or move out from it. As Kanahele explains: "The knowledge of makawalu or the movement out provides the consciousness an accurately tracking cultural progression while knowing the source of its origin." (1)

Effectively, each of the houses of knowledge is a papakū. The action of identifying and extracting the components that derive from the papakū is called makawalu. In turn, the components will become a papakū from which other components can be pulled out and examined. The Papakū Makawalu process can be infinite, it can identify multiple perspectives of the same subject. Often, a papakū can be found in each of the three Papa houses of knowledge. When the three papa converge on a single topic, a comprehensive view is revealed with potentially a fuller understanding because of multiple perspectives. Papakū Makawalu affords researchers a methodology for analyzing details and provides educators with a pedagogy that can be used to teach any Hawaiian topic, practice, or subject from many perspectives. The multiplicity of perspectives is in effect a very holistic approach to how the Hawaiian ancestors understood the nuances, socioecology, and natural cycles of their environment. My use of the term "socioecology" here is to highlight that Hawaiians did not just notice the interactions among other species around them, but also included their interactions among themselves, with other species, and also with their environment.

Deconstructing the components out from a subject is a methodical process for detailed analysis. The subject that is being deconstructed is called the papakū. The process of deconstructing out of the papakū is called makawalu. Each deconstructed component has the potential to become its own papakū with elements that can also be further identified and subsequently deconstructed as well. Essentially, every papakū can be makawalu ʻia, which means that the papakū can be deconstructed and reconstructed into several different papakū. The nuances and unknown details of any subject can be uncovered and examined through this makawalu process, which provides a methodology for analytical interpretation and a pedagogical process for didactic learning.

Papahulihonua: E makawalu iā Papahulihonua. Let us makawalu Papahulihonua. Papahulihonua will be the original papakū. First, the components of Papahulihonua are identified and then separated out. Some of the identified components for Papahulihonua are hydrology, oceanography, geology, geography, and volcanology. These components are the core composition of the Papahulihonua house of knowledge. As mentioned previously, each component can now become its own papakū, and be makawalu ʻia, deconstructed, further to attain deeper understanding of the Papahulihonua subject as a whole. The makawalu process can continue on and on.

Papahulilani: E makawalu iā Papahulilani. The identified components for Papahulilani are the sun, moon, stars, weather, and time. These components are fundamentally the core composition of the Papahulilani house of knowledge. Each component is a part of the natural process or phenomenon that exists or occurs in the atmosphere.

For example, lā, the sun, contains many components within this single papakū. Lā can be deconstructed into a papakū called movement. Within the papakū of movement the components can be further deconstructed into vertical, which includes the daily vertical traversing of the sun from sunrise to sunset, and horizontal, which includes the annual movement of the sun from the northern to the southern hemispheres of the Earth. These are natural phenomena specific to the sun observed by Hawaiians in the past and observed by Hawaiians today. Again, each of these components can become its own papakū and the makawalu process can continue on and on. Like the format of a genealogy, the process can be reversed and traced back to its very beginnings or to its original papakū.

Papanuihānaumoku: E makawalu iā Papanuihānaumoku. The final primary papakū to makawalu is Papanuihānaumoku. Papanuihānaumoku is the largest house of knowledge due to the vast amount of living organisms that reside upon this planet, specifically in Hawaiʻi and its surrounding ocean. The identified components of Papanuihānaumoku are marine organisms, plant life, insects, birds, mammals, and humans. Any living thing that goes through a reproduction or birthing process belongs to the Papanuihānaumoku house of knowledge.

Marine organisms contain many, many more components. This papakū can be makawalu ʻia, deconstructed, into coral, seaweed, invertebrates, and vertebrates. Each of these papakū can be further makawalu ʻia into more components for further examination and analysis.

The Papakū Makawalu process is a holistic understanding of a single papakū, achieved when its components are deconstructed, examined, and reconstructed. The result is an ontological map of the Hawaiian Universe. The potential for expanding the information on a single topic is unlimited. This is best expressed in a common proverb often used to say that not all knowledge comes from a single school or a single source: ʻAʻohe pau ka ʻike i ka hālau hoʻokahi (Pukui 1983, 24). For me, through the Papakū Makawalu process, this proverb has a more profound meaning, that knowledge is infinite from within a single source.

Nā Papa—Papakū Makawalu Practitioners

Papakū Makawalu is the term that Kanahele created to name the process within chants like the Kumulipo. The ability to recognize and understand that chants and stories have multiple meanings, images, and references is indeed a Hawaiian epistemology. Kanahele named the process with the intention of assisting Hawaiian practitioners by articulating an ancient methodology ingrained within Hawaiian ancestral memory.

Like Haumea in wā thirteen of the Kumulipo, Kanahele intentionally sought out members of her family or Hawaiian women who were already working in the Hawaiian educational field, were practitioners in different Hawaiian rituals and customs, were fluent in conversational Hawaiian as well as poetic Hawaiian, and had a propensity toward one of the houses of knowledge. After thoughtful consideration, trial, and experimentation, three women were chosen to take on the task of studying all the components within their chosen Papa. One of the women studies everything connected to Papahulihonua, another studies everything connected to Papahulilani, and another studies everything connected to Papanuihānaumoku. Each of these women is committed to learning their chosen Papa through the Papakū Makawalu process. They form a team guided and directed by Kanahele. Open, candid discussion is encouraged between the team members to understand how a subject or a verse within a chant is pertinent to the process.

This process affords the team the ability to gain a deeper grasp of the studied content. Hawaiian chants and ceremonial prayers are utilized as the source of gathered information. The methodology is as follows:

1. Choose a subject or topic;
2. Find a chant, ceremony, or story on the topic or subject;
3. Deconstruct the chant from each of the Papa's perspective;
4. Discuss discoveries candidly; and
5. Reconstruct the information.

The result is a holistic view of a single subject from multiple perspectives, a dynamic method for rediscovering ancient wisdom and understanding Hawaiian epistemologies. Another important outcome of the process is making obscure ancient wisdom accessible and converting it into practices that can be utilized today.

Example of Papakū Makawalu

1. CHOOSE A SUBJECT OR TOPIC

The following is an example of the Papakū Makawalu process. The papakū will be wai, water. Wai will be studied from each Papa, utilizing the Papakū Makawalu process.

2. FIND A CHANT, CEREMONY, OR STORY ON THE TOPIC OR SUBJECT

The database that will be deconstructed is a traditional chant called, He Mele a Kāne:

He ui, he nīnau:	A query, a question:
E ui aku ana au iā ʻoe,	I am inquiring
Aia i hea ka wai a Kāne?	Where is the water of Kāne?
Aia i ka hikina a ka lā,	It is in the eastern sun
Puka i Haʻehaʻe;	Revealed in Haʻehaʻe
Aia i laila ka wai a Kāne.	The water of Kāne is located there.
E ui aku ana au iā ʻoe,	I am inquiring
Aia i hea ka wai a Kāne?	Where is the water of Kāne?
Aia i Kaulanakalā,	It is in the western sun
I ka pae ʻōpua i ke kai,	In the cloud banks in the ocean,
Ea mai ana ma Nihoa,	Building in Nihoa
Ma ka mole mai o Lehua;	On the foundation of Lehua
Aia i laila ka wai a Kāne.	The water of Kāne is located there.

E ui aku ana au iā ʻoe,   I am beseeching,
Aia i hea ka wai a Kāne?   Where is the water of Kāne?
Aia i ke kuahiwi, i ke kualono,   It is in the tall mountains, the ridges,
I ke awāwa, i ke kahawai;   The valleys, the streams
Aia i laila ka wai a Kāne.   The water of Kāne is located there.

E ui aku ana au iā ʻoe,   I am requesting,
Aia i hea ka wai a Kāne?   Where is the water of Kāne?
Aia i kai, i ka moana, i ke Kualau,   It is in the ocean, the deep ocean, in squalls
I ke anuenue, i ka pūnohu,   In rainbows, in red rainbows,
A i ka uakoko,   And low-lying and suspended rainbows
I ka ʻālewalewa:
Aia i laila ka wai a Kāne.   The water of Kāne is located there.

E ui aku ana au iā ʻoe,   I am soliciting,
Aia i hea ka wai a Kāne?   Where is the water of Kāne?
Aia i luna ka Wai a Kāne,   The water of Kāne is above,
I ke ao ouli, i ke ao ʻeleʻele,   In the dark clouds, in the black clouds,
I ke ao panopano,   In the thick shiny clouds,
I ke ao pōpolohua mea a Kāne lā, e!   In the purple bronze storm clouds of Kāne!
Aia i laila ka wai a Kāne.   The water of Kāne is located there.

E ui aku ana au iā ʻoe,   I am imploring,
Aia i hea ka wai a Kāne?   Where is the water of Kāne?
Aia i lalo, i ka honua,   It is below, in the earth
I ka wai hū,   Within springs,
I ka wai kau a Kāne me Kanaloa   In the depressions of Kāne and Kanaloa
He waipuna, he wai e inu,   It's pooling water, it's water to drink
He wai e mana, he wai e ola.   It's water to empower, it's water to thrive.
E ola no, ea!   Sustenance indeed! (Emerson 1990, 216)

3. DECONSTRUCT THE CHANT FROM EACH OF THE PAPA'S PERSPECTIVE

The first things extracted from this chant would be the various types of water and the locations where water can be found. Below are the lists of water that have been deconstructed into their appropriate Papa.

Papahulihonua: Water found in mountains, ridges, valleys, streams, the deep ocean. Subterranean water found in springs, ponds, and natural pools.

Papahulilani: Dew as mentioned in the morning sunrise over Haʻehaʻe in the east. Convection as mentioned in the cloud banks as the sun sets over Nīhoa and Lehua in the west. Water found in squalls, various types of rainbows, various types of rain and storm clouds.

Papanuihānaumoku: This is the ritual being performed by the kānaka in the ceremonial act of chanting this water prayer; and also the end verse, which mentions the necessity of water for sustenance by every living creature.

4. CANDID DISCUSSION ABOUT DISCOVERIES

Each team member will begin researching chants and stories from their Papa's perspective, pulling out water types, processes of water collection, water distribution, hydrology, movement of water, formation of clouds, types of rainbows, etc. Information is gathered from both ancient Hawaiian environmental knowledge and Western resources utilizing modern technologies. The team will meet periodically to discuss findings, suggest chant material to one another, or to seek guidance from Kanahele.

5. RECONSTRUCT THE INFORMATION

Team members go into the Hawaiian environment to seek out and shoot pictures or videos of the natural phenomena mentioned in the chant(s). Locations, living organisms, or natural phenomena mentioned in the chants or stories are visited to see if the phenomena can be found today in spite of change and modern-day activities. Repeatedly visiting the subjects in their natural environment, during different seasons and over long periods of time, is ultimately the best method for becoming extremely familiar with the subject.

Once the team members have a collection of materials, pictures, and discussions of the deconstructed materials, they can reconstruct the collected material into PowerPoint presentations. This information will be presented at workshops, symposiums, and training sessions where Hawaiian practitioners, curriculum developers, teachers, college professors, resource managers, economists, and community leaders can learn the Papakū Makawalu process.

ʻIke Maka A Hoʻohana ʻIa—Application

Ideally, the Papakū Makawalu process works best for the Hawaiian researcher who has been engaging with the Hawaiian environment for long periods of time by means of traditional practices and customs passed down from one generation to the next. Intentionally investing time and repeated engagement with the natural Hawaiian environment over decades is necessary in order to begin building a foundation of environmental comprehension. A researcher in the Papakū Makawalu team must have fluency in the Hawaiian language, poetry, and customary use of language. These skills are significant for accessing and understanding traditional Hawaiian chants and stories. A commanding grasp of Hawaiian metaphor and traditional allegory is also crucial, which assists in building the imagery that allows for the creative results of deconstructing topics. A Papakū Makawalu researcher must have extensive applicable practice, that is, years of working in the environment. The resulting curriculum is not just studied for academic purposes but can be applied immediately and practiced.

Papakū Makawalu has also become the mechanism by which modern Hawaiians who have not been practicing family traditions are reestablishing connections to the natural cycles and phenomena of Hawaiʻi. Ultimately, learning the process connects the modern Hawaiian to family traditions, granting understanding of ancient practices that are valuable and particularly applicable today.

Curriculum material, visual arts, and resource management plans have been developed using the Papakū Makawalu process with the intention of reconnecting the modern Hawaiian to the past. Papakū Makawalu is a dynamic process that provides a holistic perspective of the Hawaiian Universe grounded in traditional Hawaiian epistemologies, utilizing modern-day technologies to move forward into the future.

Notes

1. Pualani Kanakaʻole Kanahele is a Kumu Hula (Master hula teacher), a Kāne practitioner, and an accomplished writer, researcher, educator, community leader, and public speaker. Kanahele currently leads a team of researchers in reestablishing an ancient Hawaiian system of cultural intelligence. The team works on resurrecting traditional knowledge ranging from ethno-astronomy to volcanism, https://www.edithkanakaolefoundation.org/publications/.

2. Papakū Makawalu workshop, February 14, 2009, Keauhou Outrigger Hotel, Kahaluʻu, Kailua-Kona, HI.

Bibliography

Beckwith, Martha W. 1951. *The Kumulipo: A Hawaiian Creation Chant.* Chicago: University of Chicago Press.

Emerson, Nathaniel B. 1998. *Unwritten Literature of Hawaiʻi. Sacred Songs of the Hula.* Honolulu: Mutual Publishing.

Johnson, Rubelite K. K. 2000. *The Kumulipo Mind: A Global Heritage. In the Polynesian Creation Myth.* Unpublished manuscript.

Kanahele, Pualani Kanakaʻole. 2011. *Ka Honua Ola, ʻEliʻeli Kau Mai.* Honolulu: Kamehameha Publishing.

Kanahele, Pualani. 2014. *Papakū Makawalu. Current Projects.* Edith Kanakaʻole Foundation, 14 February. https://www.edithkanakaolefoundation.org/current-projects/papaku-makawalu.

Papakū Makawalu Educators' Workshop. 2009. Conducted at the Outrigger Keauhou Hotel, Kahaluʻu, Kailua-Kona, HI. February 14.

Pukui, Mary K. 1983. *ʻŌlelo Noʻeau. Hawaiian Proverbs and Political Sayings.* Honolulu: Bishop Museum Press.

4

E HO‘I I KA PIKO
(RETURNING TO THE CENTER)

Theorizing Moʻokūʻauhau as Methodology in an
Indigenous Literary Context

KUʻUALOHA HOʻOMANAWANUI

> "ʻO ka moʻokūʻauhau nō ia." (The genealogy. Always, the genealogy.)
>
> *Sarah Rebekah Daniels*

In 2014, the Hawaiian voyaging canoes *Hōkūleʻa* and *Hikianalia* embarked on an epic and perhaps unprecedented four-year-long quest to circumnavigate the globe in traditionally built waʻa (canoes, vessels), using only traditional, Indigenous voyaging methods. Their central message continues to be Mālama Honua (cherishing our island earth, including one another), to "care for Island Earth, our natural environment, children, and all of humankind."[1] They are doing this through voyaging, an ancient method of transportation and knowledge across Oceania renewed and still relevant in the twenty-first century. The first stop on their journey was the islands of Tahiti,[2] the geographic, cultural, and genealogical piko (navel) for Kānaka Maoli[3] (Native Hawaiians), an integral touchstone to our ancient kūpuna (ancestors) and ancestral lands. Looking back, i ka wā ma mua (the past; lit. the time that came before), in order to ascertain pono (just, harmonious) action for ke ao nei (the present) and ka wā ma hope (future; lit. the time to come later) is an important concept in Kanaka Maoli culture. In this sense, it is e ho'i i ka piko (returning to the center), the piko representing the point of origin that is equally relevant and critical. The voyage is a visible effort meant to "inspire communities around the world to think like an islander about our [natural] resources and our relationship to these resources."[4] It is also a reminder that "the sea is our pathway to each other and to everyone else," of the power of Indigenous knowledge, practices, and connections between us, a lesson relevant and applicable to other contexts, including academia.[5]

Mo'okū'auhau, or genealogy, is a central, integral cultural concept that underpins Kanaka Maoli society, community and culture, past and present. As such, it is adaptable to other culturally derived applications aside from just recounting one's personal ancestry. This essay examines mo'okū'auhau as a methodology relevant to the study of literature as part of the wider and growing field of Indigenous Studies.

The blossoming of Indigenous Studies over the past two decades has included calls for the increased articulation and application of relevant, culturally based theories and methodologies across scholarly disciplines in the arts, sciences, humanities, and beyond. In this process, many Indigenous scholars and our supporters have cautioned against a pan-Indigenous "one size fits all" approach, and for scholars and researchers to seek and utilize more culturally specific contexts. Thus, this essay examines the Hawaiian cultural practice of mo'okū'auhau as a critical, culturally based Indigenous methodology. While I focus specifically on the discipline of literary studies and apply this approach to texts, it is an approach that is relevant to and useful in other academic disciplines as well. I argue that Indigenous, culturally located and derived methodologies, such as mo'okū'auhau, are valid within the academy and our home communities. They are also long-standing analytical and intellectual tools used for countless generations within the context of Indigenous education and our intellectual traditions; rather than new creations, they are being rediscovered, recognized, and utilized by new generations of Indigenous scholars as a way of doing Western scholarship with Indigenous tools.

I ka 'Ōlelo ke Ola (In the Language Is Life—Defining Key Terms)

I ka 'ōlelo ke ola, i ka 'ōlelo ka make, "In language is the power of life and death," is a well-known 'ōlelo no'eau (proverb) that speaks to the potent power of language, inclusive of defining and using words and terms. Thus, it is important to question the process of defining an Indigenous methodology (What is an Indigenous methodology?), understanding mo'okū'auhau in this context (How is mo'okū'auhau an example of one? How does it relate to the study of literature?), and analyzing English, Hawaiian, and other words and phrases used because language is always directly linked to people, their culture, traditions, and history.[6] In this section, I examine the key terms associated with moʻokūʻauhau as an Indigenous methodology in relation to Hawaiian literature: literature, moʻolelo, Indigenous, methodology, moʻokūʻauhau, piko, hīpuʻu (critical intersection), and makawalu (multiple perspectives).

Generally speaking, *literature*, derived from the Latin *litteratura* (involving letters, writing), is written works, including stories, novels, short stories, plays, and poetry, thought to be "valued for superior or lasting artistic merit."[7] Because of the hierarchy of meaning and value (or connotations) that get attached to literature, it is the most common (although not the most applicable) term used to describe Hawaiian literary production. Within an ʻŌiwi framework, *moʻolelo* is a broad category encompassing myriad genres of composition, both oral and written, that is inclusive of narratives such as stories and histories, which are sometimes told in other forms, such as poetry (mele or songs, poems; oli or chants, moʻokūʻauhau or genealogies, koʻihonua or genealogies recounting the creation of land). From a Western perspective, *Hawaiian literature* is synonymous with *moʻolelo Hawaiʻi*, the stories and histories, in oral tradition and writing, composed by Kānaka Maoli. But the English-derived Hawaiian literature lacks the cultural framework and historicizing element *moʻolelo Hawaiʻi* suggests:

> "Hawaiian literature" (often referred to in Hawaiʻi as "Local" literature) is not [exactly] the same as moʻolelo Hawaiʻi (a general category for literature written by Kanaka Maoli). As treasured "hi/stories" (histories + stories) mai ka pō mai [from the ancient past], mai nā kūpuna mai [from the ancestors], moʻolelo kuʻuna are traditional stories that are one strand of moʻolelo Hawaiʻi; moʻolelo kuʻuna have a genealogy and history that precedes (and supersedes) written, contemporary literature, in part because it informs (at least) or is the foundation (at best) of it.[8]

Moreover, as Larry Kauanoe Kimura argues, Hawaiian language asserts itself in creating meanings and relationships of meaning that English does not, and vice versa. Thus, in this and other work, "I purposefully utilize Hawaiian-language terms as a strategy of reasserting an Indigenous authority over our oral and literary traditions. Ngugı wa Thiongʻo reminds us that language is a carrier of culture, and Kimura writes extensively about this within a Hawaiian context."[9] This is true within a Latin-derived English context, as W. F. Nicolaisen writes, as

> Etymological, *story*, together with its close neighbor *history*, has emerged . . . [from] Latin *historia* and its Greek precursor, in their triple meaning of "learning or knowledge by inquiry, narrative,

and history," derive from *histōr* "knowing, learned, wise man, judge" which, as an earlier *idtōr*, is formed on the root *id*—"to know" which still carries that meaning in Modern German *wissen* and once did in Old English *witan*. In a wider sense, the same root has also given us, via Greek and Latin, our English words *idea* and *vision*, respectively. Here then we encounter *story* not only as narration from knowledge and wisdom but also as narrative given shape through ideas and relevance through vision.

As its English twin cognate history indicates, story is intimately and irrevocably concerned with the past . . . as it is very likely to have been; for through story we create the past, or at least significant and manageable chunks of it, and that not only in temporal frameworks but also in spatial settings . . . the past does not exist as place or time until it has been narrated through story. That is why, in so many societies and communities, the storyteller is also the historian. . . . *Story*, like naming, for example, is therefore an ubiquitous phenomenon, and *storying* one of the essential components of our intellectual survival kit. Perhaps that is the secret reason why we are not only satisfied with story as an explanation but clamor for it, even in the face of the unreliability, troublesomeness and foolishness of the word. *Story* inevitably fictionalizes while always telling the truth.[10]

Far too often written literature is assumed to be superior (and thus preferable) to oral tradition, particularly when an "authoritative" source is desired. Yet a mo'okū'auhau methodology connects orature and literature, and both a mo'okū'auhau methodology and a makawalu discourse (discussed below) demonstrate how multiple versions and variants of mo'olelo are not just acceptable, but perhaps preferable, as it allows for an array of possibilities through the analysis of several perspectives and sources of knowledge in the telling and recording of story. Thus, when discussing Hawaiian literature, or mo'olelo, the oral sources and variations of "oral text" are always implied alongside the written.

Indigenous comes from the Latin *indigenus*, "born in a country, native; born or produced naturally in a land or region; native or belonging naturally *to* (the soil, region, etc.)"; it is primarily applied to aboriginal or "first nation" inhabitants of a place.[11] Synonyms include native, original, and aboriginal; in an 'Ōiwi context, words such as kupa (citizen, familiar, native) and kama'āina (lit. child of the land) reflect the idea of "being born in a land or region." However, more specific terms, such as maoli (native, Indigenous, real, true) and 'ōiwi (native; lit. of the bones) delineate an ethnic and thus genealogically based heritage. The increased importance placed on Indigenous designations of people, place, and culture over the past decades reflects the political struggles and contestation over control of each, as both Indigenous and settler populations seek to define such power dynamics.

Within a Kanaka Maoli context, traditional moʻolelo recount our origins as being descendants of our Earth Mother, Papahānaumoku, and Sky Father, Wākea; thus, Kānaka Maoli are the Indigenous population of the Hawaiian islands. Our names for ourselves, Kanaka Maoli, ʻŌiwi, and Hawaiʻi are reflective of the primacy of moʻokūʻauhau in our worldview and its connection to our ʻāina (land; but also, like here, referring to the wider environment, including ocean and sky; lit. that which feeds). In this way, moʻokūʻauhau is an integral, traditional cultural practice making it an Indigenous, Kanaka Maoli methodology.

Most simply defined, *methodology* is "the theory of method, or the approach or technique being taken, or the reasoning for selecting a set of methods."[12] Elaborating further, Māori scholar Linda Tuhiwai Smith explains, "methodology [is] . . . not just the methods you use, but the reasoning behind them; [they are] the set of underlying principles that inform research."[13] In other words, it is both the how and the why of presenting knowledge. Within an Indigenous framework, these questions are rooted in a cultural foundation.

Moʻokūʻauhau is genealogy; "in its narrowest sense, [it] refers to biological lineage,"[14] and is inclusive of "a genealogical relationship" that is applicable "to people and living things."[15] As such, it is "the genealogical starting point of all things Hawaiian," the piko (center, navel, origin, point of origin), if you will.[16]

> One meaning of the root word <u>moʻo</u> is "series or succession"; <u>kū</u> has myriad meanings, including to stand, resemble, reveal, transform and rule the land, while one definition of ʻ<u>auhau</u> references the leg bones [Elbert and Pukui, *Hawaiian Dictionary*, pp. 31, 167]. One way of understanding moʻokūʻauhau is the succession of generations standing on the bones of the ancestors.[17]

The succession of generations is, in part, about connection—connecting to one's ancestors and their wisdom; it is about connecting to the ʻāina, about understanding and embracing one's cultural worldview. Thus, it is the underlying principle, as Tuhiwai Smith argues, of who we are as Kanaka Maoli, and in this way is integral to our research ethics. Numerous ʻŌiwi scholars have established the primacy and importance of Indigenous Hawaiian perspectives in general, and moʻokūʻauhau in particular, in their groundbreaking work in diverse academic fields.[18]

In *Voices of Fire, Reweaving the Literary Lei of Pele and Hiʻiaka* (2014), I argue that moʻokūʻauhau is central to understanding the relationship between the myriad versions of the Pele and Hiʻiaka epics published between

1860 and 1928. As mo'okū'auhau they "describe the relationship between texts with the intentional connotation of a genealogical succession. This relationship is multidimensional—the texts both represent the writers, editors, and islands they are from."[19] By viewing the archive of texts as a collective with an intellectual and cultural relationship between them, rather than just as individual texts, allows for a different kind of reading, interpretation, and understanding of them beyond "just" literature, creative stories with the sole (or most important) purpose of entertainment. Rather,

> Collectively they kept the mo'olelo alive and at the forefront of the Hawaiian national consciousness, successfully transforming the vibrant oral narrative to a robust literary form. Thus, a relationship of cultural and historical production and reception is also implied; mo'okū'auhau suggests a level of kuleana inherent in Hawaiian practice, a Hawaiian expression of what [Robert] Warrior calls an intellectual tradition.[20]

This intellectual tradition springs from the oral tradition, which I call the piko for written Hawaiian literature.[21] Kiowa writer N. Scott Momaday is just one of many Indigenous literature scholars who recognize oral tradition (sometimes called oral literature or orature) as "the foundation of literature."[22] In a Hawaiian context, this piko of oral tradition has been passed down over time mai nā kūpuna mai (from the ancestors to us), first in oral traditions that include inoa (names) and performances of various genres of oli (chant), mele (song), hula (dance), pule (prayer), ha'i mo'olelo (storytelling), ha'i mo'okū'auhau (recitation of genealogies), and kanikau (laments). Later, these and other genres of artistic and cultural expression were recorded and composed on paper and transformed to include ka palapala (written literature).

Piko is the navel, the connection point linking mother and child, one generation to the next. The kalo (taro) plant provides an important example: the piko is the heart of the lau kalo (taro leaf) that connects it to hā (stem) down to the kalo (corm); the mid-stalk and kōhina (corm crown) is called the huli (overturn; a regeneration), the part replanted to continue the next generation. The kalo is the physical representation of Hāloa, the elder kalo-bodied sibling and elemental ancestor of Kanaka 'Ōiwi, the piko of our cultural mo'okū'auhau, the 'ohā (kalo shoots; fig. offspring), the root for 'ohana (family), the lau (leaf) suggested in the word lāhui (people, nation; lit. lā-, contraction of lau, hui, to gather).

Piko is also a center, not always of space or time, but metaphorically. The center of a fishing net is called the piko; like a mo'okū'auhau, the strands unfurl out in time and space, and are linked by hīpu'u, secured knots that provide strength and stability, linking points from one entity to the next. In this way, each island across Oceania is a hīpuʻu; each generation born, connected through the piko is a hīpuʻu. We might imagine, as a multiple-perspective makawalu discourse allows us, to see each native origin story as a piko, linking in to other moʻokūʻauhau via hīpuʻu of genealogy, intellectual history, cultural practice, and (even) methodology. Within the context of literary studies, hīpuʻu are the critical intersections linking strands of moʻokūʻauhau, manaʻo (thoughts, ideas), moʻolelo (texts), and so forth, originating in the piko of tradition, mai ka pō mai, mai nā kūpuna mai.

Makawalu literally means "eight eyes," and relates to multiple perspectives, to seeing different and sometimes opposing views. It complements other ʻōlelo noʻeau that speak to the acceptance of diverse viewpoints, and embrace the depth and breadth of ʻŌiwi intellectual wisdom and artistry, such as ʻaʻole pau ka ʻike i ka hālau hoʻokahi (not all knowledge is contained in one school). Makawalu "also facilitates the cultural concept of ka ʻimi loa, long-standing (life-long), in-depth research and exploration of knowledge with a goal of mastery for preservation and education of others with an eye on future generations."[23] Makawalu is relevant to moʻokūʻauhau as methodology because it allows us to see multiple strands and layering of moʻokūʻauhau as important in the study of Hawaiian literature. It allows us to understand and unlock meaning within texts, as well as see the influence of the cultural, social, political, historical, linguistic, economic, and other influences on an author, on how a text may have been conceived, what conditions it was born into, how it is perceived in our time, and how it might be received and understood in the future.

Moʻokūʻauhau as Methodology

In "Ka Liʻu o ka Paʻakai (Well Seasoned with Salt): Recognizing Literary Devices, Rhetorical Strategies and Aesthetics in Kanaka Maoli Literature" (2015), I discuss the importance of moʻokūʻauhau as a meiwi, or an ethnopoetic rhetorical and literary device in Hawaiian moʻolelo. As a meiwi, the positioning of a moʻokūʻauhau at the very beginning of a moʻolelo frames the narrative in particular ways because it is an ʻŌiwi way of expressing knowledge within moʻolelo (story, history, or scholarship). In many Hawaiian texts—oral and written, in the past and present, and in traditional moʻolelo and academic scholarship—the moʻokūʻauhau of the primary figure(s) is often prominently featured at the very beginning of the narrative. The recitation of a moʻokūʻauhau, however brief, often alludes to (if it doesn't outright state) the speaker's lineage, place of birth, and place of residence.

In doing so, the speaker's kuleana (right, responsibility) to speak, and their knowledge of the subject at hand, as well as their kūlana (place, stance, and reputation, suggesting accountability) is also brought into play. Such references also evoke kaona, or metaphoric and multiple layers of meaning, not necessarily ascertained by all audience members or readers. In this way, it is also a method demonstrating knowledge and establishing authority (kuleana, kūlana) that extends beyond how and why, but also includes *who* as voice and also as subject. A mo'okū'auhau methodology is the recognition and application of mo'okū'auhau as part of a larger set of procedures for analysis and interpretation that function on multiple levels, including focusing the audience's attention in a particular way, providing not just a reason for telling the mo'olelo, but also demonstrating the writer's knowledge and thus credibility in relaying such information, as well as demonstrating how other people (writers, scholars) have used it to establish authority over the text(s), and making connections between writers, publications, and texts not possible without such an approach.[24] This occurs in multiple ways, calling for further delineation of types of mo'okū'auhau, such as pili koko (blood relations), 'ike (knowledge), and hālau 'ike (disciplinary; lit. schools of knowledge).

Mo'okū'auhau pili koko, mo'okū'auhau 'ike

Mo'okū'auhau pili koko (lit. blood relation genealogy) specifically identifies a blood relative and blood relationship or familial lineage, the primary application and understanding of mo'okū'auhau as a concept. It is the cultural foundation for mo'okū'auhau 'ike (lit. knowledge genealogy) and mo'okū'auhau hālau 'ike (disciplinary genealogies; lit. schools of knowledge).

Within mo'olelo Hawai'i, the first application of mo'okū'auhau as genealogy is pili koko, a familial one recounting the ancestry and genealogical ties of the main figure(s). In mo'olelo ku'una, genealogies of primary characters are often given in the introductory paragraphs. In various accounts of Pele and Hi'iaka, several differing versions of their mo'okū'auhau are provided.[25] Similarly, the story of 'A'ahoaka, a kupua (extraordinary figure, culture hero) of Puna, Kaua'i, born to the Keālia-based ali'i (chief) Kalalea (his father) and Koananai (his mother) begins with his parents' lineages, including mention of his mother's older eel brother and sister, and his paternal grandfather Kapaopao, an ali'i of the region.[26] This is also true in historical and life writing narratives, such as the story of Kaua'i paniolo (cowboy) Kaluaiko'olau, who became well known in the 1890s after he contracted leprosy and was ordered to the Kalawao settlement on the island of Moloka'i, but refused to leave his wife, child, and homeland behind. After shooting and killing the local sheriff sent to capture and force his exile to Moloka'i, the Provisional Government, led by those responsible for the overthrow of the Hawaiian kingdom in 1893, sent their army to Kaua'i to capture him, without success.[27] After a lengthy oli aloha (chant of greeting), the mo'olelo of Ko'olau's life begins with his and his wife Pi'ilani's mo'okū'auhau pili koko.[28] Similarly, the biography of Robert William Kalanihiapo Wilcox begins with his birth, place of birth (Kahului, Honua'ula, Maui), short account of his immediate moʻokūʻauhau (provided in detail later in the text) and a description of his ʻano (character) that foreshadows his illustrious adulthood and aliʻi status proclaimed in his Hawaiian name Kalanihiapo (the royal eldest child).[29]

While these uses of moʻokūʻauhau pili koko function as meiwi (ethno-poetic rhetoric and literary devices),[30] they are also methods or tools used by the writers to demonstrate their authority over the subject, and their cultural knowledge of how to appropriately convey a narrative using ʻŌiwi aesthetics. On another level, they are methodologies because they are part of a larger set of procedures of analysis and interpretation that function on multiple levels.

This methodological use of moʻokūʻauhau is found in the literary and historical works of other ʻŌiwi writers, such as Samuel Manaiakalani Kamakau's works on Hawaiian history, and the historical writings of John Papa ʻĪʻī.[31] As Brown discusses in her dissertation, "moʻokūʻauhau is a conspicuous thread throughout ʻĪʻī's series. In addition to his explanations of his own lineage, he offers extensive genealogical information for others."[32] Kamakau's, ʻĪʻī's, and others' use of moʻokūʻauhau represents a moʻokūʻauhau methodology because of how and why they present knowledge. Within an Indigenous framework, these questions are rooted in a cultural foundation important to a Hawaiian audience, and important in their creation and maintenance of ʻŌiwi aesthetics and ethos.

At another level, moʻokūʻauhau is a methodology for scholars to recognize its use within moʻolelo, and in establishing their own research kuleana, kūlana, and moʻokūʻauhau as part of the thought process and underlying principles informing our research. This is the cultural foundation of our intellectual history as ʻŌiwi scholars, or at least is something we should be striving toward.

Moʻokūʻauhau as methodology extends to pili koko relationships outside of the moʻolelo as well, such as the writers, authors, poets, composers, publishers, and editors involved in the creation and publication of a text. Applying a moʻokūʻauhau methodology this way raises many important research questions. Using the textual examples already provided, one could ask, using this methodology: Who published the story of ʻAʻahoaka? Why did the newspaper, publisher, and writer publish it? What is their kuleana and kūlana to do so? What about Kelekona? Kamakau? ʻĪʻī? Nakanaela? Are their moʻokūʻauhau pili koko important to research? Does it determine what they know, how they know it, and how they have kuleana and kūlana to share it? What role does their moʻokūʻauhau pili koko play in relation to their moʻokūʻauhau ʻike (genealogies of knowledge)? Is it a matter of ancestral or cultural memory, a training process (hālau ʻike) with knowledge passed down over generations, or both?

Moʻokūʻauhau pili koko often includes references to places of birth (one hānau), residence (wahi noho), or ancestral homelands (kulaiwi), which can also be reflected in personal and ancestral names within the moʻokūʻauhau.

There are various ways such information is presented in mo'olelo: often the place of birth is provided, sometimes this explains the naming of people for places, or places for people. For example, 'A'ahoaka is the name of a pyramid-shaped hill located between the north and south branches of the Wailua River; Kalalea is the name of a prominent dorsal-fin-shaped peak on the main mountain in Anahola; and Koananai is the name of the other large, rounded peak on the southern end of the mountain range. Other senior relatives on both sides of his mo'okū'auhau area also named for important Kaua'i locations, or have these locations named for them, including his paternal grandmother, Kāhala (point, Anahola), and Kua'ehu (point, Aliomanu bay, Anahola), an advisor to his grandfather Kapaopao.[33]

In *Kaluaiko'olau*, the locations of Ko'olau and Pi'ilani's births, as well as the hō'ailona (signs, omens) and circumstances accompanying their births are also provided. Moreover, detailed place-names of where they stayed while they were traveling to and from Kalalau valley, as well as places they lived there, are also provided. More importantly, the relationships between these places, and Pi'ilani's oli aloha (chant of affection) for them upon her leaving Kalalau for the last time, are key details within the mo'olelo.[34] Subsequently, this promotes a mo'okū'auhau of knowledge, as such place-names and their connection to Kanaka 'Ōiwi are not always found in common reference sources such as *Place Names of Hawaii* or the more recent *Hawai'i Place names*—Koananai and Kua'ehu, for example, are not mentioned in either of these important reference sources. Instead, they are found in the mo'olelo of 'A'ahoaka and others.[35] Of sixteen place-names in Pi'ilani's oli aloha, eleven are not found in *Place Names of Hawaii* or *Hawai'i Place Names*.[36]

In her discussion of linguistic mapping of Native space in oral traditions, Brooks argues that place-names and their relationships to each other for the Abernaki are "not fully documented by historians, [even though] all of these places are well known in Abernaki oral traditions as areas where families gathered during the nineteenth century."[37] In this way, the mo'olelo or literary context becomes more important, as they are often the only sources that contain such knowledge, and the genealogy of such knowledge. For 'Ōiwi, such relationships to place are often an integral part of one's mo'okū'auhau, a mo'okū'auhau pili 'āina (genealogy connecting one to specific places, of birth, residence, or ancestry) often directly linked to mo'okū'auhau 'āina (genealogy of land). Mo'okū'auhau pili 'āina also reflect mo'okū'auhau 'ike and mo'okū'auhau hālau 'ike.

Mainstream academic scholarship does not require or even discuss the importance of one's personal mo'okū'auhau in undertaking research in any discipline. Thus, inclusion of a personal mo'okū'auhau is not necessary to conduct literary (or other) scholarship. However, for scholars who advocate for Indigenous perspectives and methodologies in our own work and across our disciplines, inclusion of such practices, like mo'okū'auhau, is important and central. In my own work I follow and strongly advocate for a reflective examination of one's own moʻokūʻauhau in academic study, if for no other reason, to help us better focus on how we are approaching our topics. In some cases, our moʻokūʻauhau can determine a kūlana for our work; in the field of literature, it can influence why we choose particular texts, or how we read them. Having a genealogical connection to texts or authors can also provide certain insights to the work that others may not have. Not having a personal connection to texts or writers does not preclude us from studying the literature. Rather, it can make us more attuned to approach the text with a sensitivity and respect we might not otherwise have, and to understand our kūlana and kuleana as researchers. It is important to ask ourselves, before we commence any project, what is my personal moʻokūʻauhau, and how does it connect me to (do) this work?

This link between moʻokūʻauhau and kuleana is not new. Historian Kanalu Young addresses the role of haku (lord, master) as "still largely determined by the longstanding personal and family relationships between high chiefs and chiefly servers through the nineteenth century," even as the new forms of government based on Western models "confuse[d] the matter of [traditional] lines of authority."[38] As Marie Alohalani Brown argues in her dissertation on the life of John Papa ʻĪʻī, his service (kuleana) to the Kamehamehas directly correlates with his moʻokūʻauhau:

> [ʻĪʻī's] service is directly related to kuleana. ʻĪʻī's kuleana was informed by his genealogy and by his parents' wishes for him. Because of ʻĪʻī's role as a kahu [guardian] to the highest-ranking chiefs during and throughout his lifetime, and because his role evolved to match the changing times, his life offers insights into the kinds of service lower-ranking chiefs could and did provide the governing aliʻi.[39]

If moʻokūʻauhau is related to the role of kaukau aliʻi who served the higher ranking aliʻi, then it serves as a cultural model for understanding our roles today in modern professions in service to the lāhui (nation, people), such as in academia. Thus, another aspect of our personal moʻokūʻauhau that is important to consider is one's disciplinary or academic genealogy. The schools where we study determine which professors, scholars, and researchers we work with; they become part of our academic moʻokūʻauhau through their mentoring. Moreover, the disciplines we study and practice in, as well as the time period we are studying in, also influence the theories and methodologies we are exposed to, and those we eschew and espouse. Our academic fields train us to do research in certain ways, to privilege some theories, and types of research strategies—including methodologies—over others. Some helpful questions to ask include: What school(s) have I studied in? Who have I worked with? Who have I read? What theories and methodologies have I been exposed to? How does my training influence how I am approaching this work/these texts?

I've discussed this in my own work on Pele and Hi'iaka literature, recounting my genealogical connections to Pele's lands of Puna and Ka'ū, Hawai'i; my paternal grandmother's 'ohana are from Kapa'ahu in Puna, the place where Pele slept, wrapped in an 'ahu (cloak) of kapa cloth, hence the name of this important wahi pana (place made famous through story), Kapa'ahu (cloak made of kapa). I also discuss my hālau hula (hula school) training under kumu (teacher) John Ka'imikaua. Kumu Ka'imikaua practiced the tradition of Moloka'i as the hula piko (navel of hula), with Pele's other sisters Kapō'ulakīna'u and Kewelani (Laka) as the primary hula deities, which is different from those who trace their hula lineage back to Pele's other sister Hi'iakaikapoliopele and her love Hōpoe in Puna, Hawai'i.[40] As a scholar trained in the disciplines of Hawaiian Studies (with Hawaiian language as a requirement), Polynesian Religion, and English (Cultural Studies, Literary Studies), I approach Hawaiian texts with a sensitivity to Hawaiian language and issues of translation, an attention to kaona, and a strong desire to uncover the cultural, social, and political meanings of a text, and the implications of the production of the text, that I might not have if I had been trained in another field. All of these aspects of my personal and professional mo'okū'auhau are important to which mo'olelo I study and how I approach them. They also influence how I understand and write about a text, which differs from those who are not Kānaka Maoli, do not have a Hawaiian language background, and/or who are trained in other disciplines.

Similarly, Indigenous Literary Nationalism began blossoming in Native American Studies in the late 1990s—early 2000s when I was a graduate student. While not a direct part of my graduate studies, its relevance to my work in Hawaiian literature was undeniable. Works by scholars such as Robert Warrior, Jace Weaver, Craig Womack, Daniel Justice, Lisa Brooks, Greg Sarris, and others became key to developing my mo'okū'auhau 'ike in a new way. It provided a new avenue for discussing the inherent politics embedded in Hawaiian literature that recognized and honored the Indigenous aspect of our literature in ways that other cultural studies theories did not, one that allowed for the assertion of mo'okū'auhau as a critical, Indigenous, scholarly methodology.

I am sometimes asked why I chose to work on the difficult project of studying and writing about thirteen separate Pele and Hi'iaka mo'olelo. I usually assert that I didn't choose it, it chose me, based in part on all of my genealogies (personal, cultural, academic) I discuss above. But it was also a wonderful example (and certainly not the only one) of texts to apply mo'okū'auhau methodology to. For example, in addition to the external mo'okū'auhau listed above, it is important to utilize mo'okū'auhau methodology in the study of the texts themselves.

Unlike Western concepts of literature, which often privilege a single, named author as the creative force behind a single text that is a work of fiction, Hawaiian moʻolelo includes oral, sometimes anonymous compositions, transcribed and/or "translated" written versions, often by a named author, and only later, beginning perhaps in the late nineteenth to early twentieth century, a single named author as the creative force behind a single text not necessarily identified as "fiction,"[41] but as derived from the oral tradition.

Discussing moʻokūʻauhau pili koko and pili ʻāina of writers, editors, and their publications (primarily newspapers) is also an important application of moʻokūʻauhau methodology. What became apparent in my decades of study of the Pele and Hiʻiaka literature is that while there are common threads, themes, characters, mele (including oli, hula, and pule) across most (but not all) of the Pele and Hiʻiaka moʻolelo, there were important differences; these differences, I argue, are ones of moʻokūʻauhau, at multiple levels. Each writer represents their own personal moʻokūʻauhau, and in extension, that of their islands or hānau (place of birth). In some cases they represent their training in hula, or other cultural practice or profession, such as kahu (caretakers) of heiau (traditional religious temple). A number of nineteenth-century writers who recorded Pele and Hiʻiaka moʻolelo in Hawaiian language newspapers were educated (Samuel Kamakau, Joseph Poepoe) and/or were aliʻi class (Emma Nakuina).

Nā Hīpuʻu ʻĒ aʻe (Other Connections): Moʻokūʻauhau as Methodology and Other Native Literatures

The opening epigraph of this chapter is a Facebook post by ʻŌiwi writer Sarah Rebekah Daniels and her response to sharing a "Map of the Week: Native American Nations."[42] The post, by Victoria Richmond, features Cherokee and Oklahoma native Aaron Carapella's "Native American Nations, Our Own Names and Locations" mapping project, which he undertook while studying Native American history, and couldn't find a comprehensive map from a Native perspective. Carapella's mapping project includes different versions of the maps that focus on different specifics for individual tribes and their lands. Such a mapping project is an important example of the genealogical linking of the people with their ʻāina.[43] Indigenous cosmologies tell us we are born from the land. Our genealogies connect us to specific lands and make each culture unique through specific stories relevant to our geographies and environments. These in turn shape our cosmologies, worldviews, and understanding of our elemental origins.

While discovery and exploration are always practices linked with Western science and colonialism, our ancestors were also discoverers and explorers. The worldwide voyage of *Hōkūleʻa* and *Hikianalia* are but one example. Moʻokūʻauhau is a culturally derived Indigenous practice/methodology that allows us to reconceptualize these terms, via genealogy, as Indigenous. On one level, it is practical: we have connections and we have journeyed out from the piko, our center of origins. On another it is metaphoric: we are who we were, we sail in the wake of our ancestors, we continue to discover, explore, and (re)create our (place in the) world.

Yet mo'okū'auhau is not exclusive to Hawaiian cultural practices, and is found in other Indigenous cultures. More recently, it is included as part of a conscious effort to forward Indigenous methodologies. For example, in *Indigenous Methodologies*, Margaret Kovach (Plains Cree, Salteaux) begins with a Prologue recounting her immediate genealogy, a purposeful introduction because "it is relational work."[44] She shares "enough about myself" because stating her genealogy is an important way to "prepare the reader for this work."[45]

References to textual genealogies in Native American literature are also not unheard of. Prominent Native American writers and literary scholars, including Kiowa M. Scott Momaday's *The Man Made of Words*, Osage Robert Warrior's *The People and the Word*, Abernaki Lisa Brooks' *The Common Pot*, and Cherokee Thomas King's *The Inconvenient Indian*, all discuss different lineages, kinships, and trajectories of various Native American textual mo'okū'auhau.

In part, mo'okū'auhau is critical across Indigenous cultures and communities because of our real world struggles with colonization and settler colonialism, which often manifest as increased poverty, dispossession from ancestral and sacred lands, and ever increasing militarization of our homelands, and in the Pacific, of our ocean. Thus, Indigenous theories and methodologies are critical because of what is at stake. Rather than just a fruitless academic exercise, the need to recognize and embody our Indigenous intellectual histories, incorporate them into our educational, social, economic, and political systems that benefit our home communities is urgent, as we collectively seek to better real-world conditions for our lāhui.

Thus, a mo'okū'auhau methodology also allows 'Ōiwi literary scholars to see the inter- (intra-) connection between mo'olelo that goes beyond the hīpu'u I discuss in *Voices of Fire*. As Lisa Brooks notes in her discussion of Indigenous Northeast oral and literary traditions, "the depth and complexity of Native oral traditions leave much room for nuanced historical and literary interpretations, in stark contrast to the simplistic Wabanaki 'myths' and 'legends' published by anthropologists and folklorists . . . *awikhigan* takes the form of a grand and sweeping narrative of communal history with interlocking stories rather than that of a collection of individual folktales, which was popular at the time."[46]

Such kinship and interconnection reflect layers of mo'okū'auhau methodology in nuanced and sophisticated ways across Indigenous literary studies and Native cultures. They remind us as well of Cherokee Chadwick Allen's call for a trans-Indigenous methodology for global Native studies. Returning to the piko, such a call evokes Mālama Honua, and the oceanic metaphor of earth as waʻa.

Haʻina ʻia mai ana ka puana (Conclusion)

Hōkūleʻa and *Hikianalia* covered over 47,000 nautical miles and visited 26 countries in the span of their epic four-year voyage. *Hōkūleʻa* initially set sail in 1975 as the first modern canoe to voyage relying upon traditional navigational techniques and knowledge. It re-established the long dormant practice of long-distance voyaging, of discovery, exploration and the creation of new knowledge. Such voyaging allows for the reconceptualization of the ocean not as a space that divides Oceania, but as our common "ground." As Tongan scholar Epeli Hauʻofa has so eloquently argued, we are not isolated "islands in a far-flung sea," but a "sea of islands" united by it.[47] This thought features in the literary collection by Kanaka Maoli writer Lisa Linn Kanae and her short story collection titled *Islands Linked by Ocean*.[48] Master ʻŌiwi navigator Nainoa Thompson has described the earth as an island, alternately as a waʻa we are all sailing together; Kanaka Maoli educators and activists such as Kaleikoa Kaʻeo have used the metaphor of waʻa in current social and political activism in Hawaiʻi to discuss both internal Kanaka Maoli political issues, as well as those targeting Pacific Islands immigrant communities.

Voyaging across the Pacific reminds us of our genealogical connection to other peoples and places, and as new links connecting ancient Pacific peoples to the continents that surround us, and as we collectively voyage through cyberspace into the twenty-first century, we will continue to forge new connections, and reinforce established ones. Moʻokūʻauhau as a literary methodology allows for the creation of new intellectual connections and trajectories of knowledge within the academy and our home communities, a continuity of intellectual scholarship born in the piko mai ka pō mai, mai nā kūpuna mai.

By returning to the piko we can understand the connection between moʻokūʻauhau as kinship and an interlinking, expansive web of connections. In extension, our genealogies of knowledge are integral to the understanding of moʻokūʻauhau as methodology as well as critical inquiry applicable to Indigenous studies, such as:

1. disciplinary/academic moʻokūʻauhau
2. moʻokūʻauhau ʻike (genealogies of knowledge—trad., hālau, academic, etc.)
3. theory/methodologies (such as Indigenous literary nationalism, queer or feminist theories, etc.)
4. subject/textual moʻokūʻauhau

5. writers being studied (representing their families, communities, islands, etc.)
6. tracing use/introduction of/change in terms, concepts, etc.

These kinds of mo'okū'auhau express other kinds of kinship relationships beyond pili koko. Moreover, this is not an exhaustive list. It is possible and perhaps preferable to consider multiple contexts and applications when utilizing a mo'okū'auhau methodology in studying literature.

Mo'okū'auhau as methodology is not a new concept. Rather, it is a continuation of our intellectual history. As Brown so eloquently summarizes, "In their complexity, mo'okū'auhau evoke to mind a majestic 'ōhi'a lehua tree, whose branches extend upward and outward, its roots hidden from our eyes beneath the ground, radiating ever outward as they creep endlessly downward. In other words, recovering genealogical information is never a straightforward task."[49] Recognizing mo'okū'auhau—establishing kuleana, making connections—and utilizing such an approach as methodology is to sail in the wake of our ancestors, to ho'i i ka piko, return to the source, of our knowledge, our inspiration.

Notes

Epigraph. Sarah Rebekah Daniels. "Genealogy." Facebook.com, June 6, 2014.

1. www.hokulea.org.
2. The canoes made first landfall at Rangiroa in the Tuamotu Islands, part of French Polynesia, before making their way to Pape'ete and Tautira on the island of Tahiti. The village of Tautira adopted *Hōkūle'a* on its maiden voyage in 1976, and the wa'a has continued stopping there on subsequent voyages.
3. Kanaka Maoli, Kanaka 'Ōiwi, Kanaka Hawai'i and 'Ōiwi Maoli are all synonymous terms for "Hawaiian" in 'ōlelo Hawai'i, our indigenous language.
4. www.nakalaiwaa.org.
5. Hau'ofa, "The Ocean in Us," 43.
6. Kimura, "Native Hawaiian Culture," 175.
7. "Literature," *Oxford English Dictionary.*
8. ho'omanawanui, *Voices of Fire,* kindle loc. 612–618.
9. Ibid.
10. Nicolaisen, "Why Tell Stories?"
11. "Indigenous," *Oxford English Dictionary.*
12. Smith, *Decolonizing Methodologies, Research and Indigenous Peoples,* kindle loc. 109.
13. Ibid.
14. Brown, "Parrying the Spears of Change," 36.
15. ho'omanawanui, *Voices of Fire,* xxxviii.
16. Kanahele, *Ka Honua Ola,* xiv.
17. ho'omanawanui, *Voices of Fire,* xxxviii.

18. See Kimura (1985), Kameʻeleihiwa (1992), Trask (1993), Young (1998), Meyer (1998, 2003, 2008), Silva (2004), Kanahele (2005, 2011), Goodyear-Kaopua (2005), Kaomea, (2006), Tengan (2008), and Kapā Oliveira (2014) for some important examples.

19. hoʻomanawanui, *Voices of Fire*, xxxviii.

20. Ibid.

21. Ibid.

22. Momaday. *The Man Made of Words*, 14.

23. hoʻomanawanui, *Voices of Fire*, xxxviii.

24. Mahalo nui loa to Lisa Uperesa for helping me further clarify these ideas.

25. See Manu (1899) and Rice (1908).

26. "He Moolelo no Aahoaka," *Ka Nupepa Kuokoa*, December 30, 1876, 1.

27. Kelekona and Koʻolau, *The True Story of Kaluaikoʻolau*.

28. Ibid., 5–6.

29. Nakanaela, *Ka Buke Moolelo o Hon. Robert William Wilikoki*, 1.

30. See Perreira "He Haʻiʻōlelo Kuʻuna," and McDougall and Nordstrom, "Ma ka Hana ka ʻIke."

31. Kamakau's work originally appeared in serialized form in several Hawaiian language newspapers as "Ka Moolelo Hawaii" (Hawaiian History), and later decontextualized and segregated into thematic publications, such as *Ruling Chiefs of Hawaii* (Kamehameha Schools, 1991). See Nogelmeier (2010) for a more in-depth discussion of Kamakau's works.

32. Brown, "Parrying the Spears of Change," 54.

33. "He Moolelo no Aahoaka."

34. Kelekona and Koʻolau, *The True Story of Kaluaikoʻolau*, 6.

35. "He Moolelo no Aahoaka."

36. These include: Kamaile, Kahalanui, Waimakemake (and stream), Kōheo, Pūneʻe, Limamuku, Kaalaneo, Kalahau, ʻOheʻoheiki, and Kaluamoi. Kekekona and Koʻolau, *The True Story of Kaluaikoʻolau*.

37. Brooks, *The Common Pot*, 249.

38. Young, *Rethinking the Native Hawaiian Past* provides the example of Kanaʻina as magistrate, which "can also be understood as an added dimension of service, something performed in addition to the traditional *hana lawelawe* role" (112). However, aliʻi "paid less and less attention to rank as years passed" because of depopulation, resulting in "more emphasis . . . placed on longevity and whoever the survivors were" (112).

39. Brown, "Parrying the Spears of Change," 27.

40. See hoʻomanawanui, *Voices of Fire*. The Molokaʻi hula tradition is detailed in Moses Manu's 1899 text, "Ke Kaua Nui Weliweli ma waena o Pelekeahialoa a me Wakakeakaikawai," *Ka Loea Kalaiaina*, May 13–December 31, 1899.

41. The typical categories applied to such texts in the Hawaiian language newspapers of the nineteenth to early twentieth centuries include moʻolelo, kaʻao, and moʻolelo kaʻao. While the *Hawaiian Dictionary* defines moʻolelo as both history and story, and kaʻao as "Legend, tale, novel, romance, usually fanciful; fiction; tell a fanciful tale," there is not always a clear-cut distinction between what is "fact" (historical moʻolelo) and what is "fiction" (moʻolelo kaʻao).

42. Richmond, "The Roundup, Map of the Week: Native American Nations." January 8, 2014. http://thislandpress.com/roundups/map-of-the-week-native-american-nations/.
43. Viewable via his website, http://tribalnationsmaps.com.
44. Kovach, *Indigenous Methodologies*, kindle loc. 59.
45. Ibid.
46. Brooks, *The Common Pot*, kindle loc. 3740.
47. Hauʻofa, "Our Sea of Islands."
48. Kanae, *Islands Linked by Ocean*.
49. Brown, "Parrying the Spears of Change," 55.

Bibliography

Allen, Chadwick. *TransIndigenous, Methodologies for Global Native Literary Studies*. Minneapolis: University of Minnesota Press, 2012.

Brooks, Lisa. *The Common Pot, the Recovery of Native Space in the Northeast*. Minneapolis: University of Minnesota Press, 2008.

Brown, Marie Alohalani. "Parrying the Spears of Change: The Life of John Papa ʻĪʻī." Diss. University of Hawaiʻi at Mānoa, 2014.

Capella, Aaron. "Native American Nations, Our Own Names and Locations." In http://thislandpress.com/roundups/map-of-the-week-native-american-nations/; http://tribalnationsmaps.com.

Clark, John R. K. *Hawaiʻi Place Names: Shores, Beaches, and Surf Sites*. Honolulu: University of Hawaiʻi Press, 2001.

Daniels, Sarah Rebekah. "Genealogy." Facebook.com, June 6, 2014.

Hauʻofa, ʻEpeli. "Our Sea of Islands." In *Inside Out: Literature, Cultural Politics, and Identity in the New Pacific*. Eds. Vilsoni Hereniko and Rob Wilson. Lanham: Rowman and Littlefield, 1999. 27–38.

——. "The Ocean in Us." *The Contemporary Pacific* 10.2 (1998): 393–410.

"He Moolelo no Aahoaka, ke Koa a me Kona Hanau Kupanaha ana." *Ka Nupepa Kuokoa*, December 30, 1876.

hoʻomanawanui, kuʻualoha. "Ka Liʻu o ka Paʻakai (Well Seasoned with Salt): Recognizing Literary Devices, Rhetorical Strategies, and Aesthetics in Kanaka Maoli Literature." In *Huihui, Navigating Art and Literature in the Pacific*. Eds. Jeff Carroll, Brandy Nālani McDougall, and Georganne Nordstrom. Honolulu: University of Hawaiʻi Press, 2015.

——. *Voices of Fire: Reweaving the Literary Lei of Pele and Hiʻiaka*. Minneapolis: University of Minnesota Press, 2014.

Kamakau, Samuel Manaiakalani. *Ruling Chiefs of Hawaiʻi*. Honolulu: Kamehameha Schools Press, 1991.

Kanae, Lisa Linn. *Islands Linked by Ocean*. Honolulu: Bamboo Ridge Press, 2009.

Kanahele, Pualani. *Ka Honua Ola, ʻEliʻeli kau mai*. Honolulu: Kamehameha Publishing, 2011.

Kelekona, Kahikina [John Sheldon], and Piʻilani Koʻolau. 1906. *The True Story of Kaluaikoʻolau*. Trans. Frances Frazier. Līhuʻe: Kauaʻi Historical Society, 2001.

King, Thomas. *The Inconvenient Indian, a Curious Account of Native People in North America*. Minneapolis: University of Minnesota Press, 2013. Kindle edition.

Kovach, Margaret. *Indigenous Methodologies, Characters, Conversations, and Contexts*. Toronto: University of Toronto Press, 2009. Kindle edition.

Manu, Moses. "He Moolelo Kaao Hawaii no ke Kaua Nui Weliweli ma waena o Pelekeahialoa a me Wakakeakaikawai." *Ka Loea Kalaiaina*, May 13–December 31, 1899.

McDougall, Brandy Nālani, and Georganne Nordstrom. "Ma ka Hana ka ʻIke (In the Work Is the Knowledge): Kaona as Rhetorical Action." *College Composition and Communication* 63.1 (September 2011): 98–121.

Momaday, N. Scott. *The Man Made of Words: Essays, Stories, Passages*. New York: St. Martin's Press, 1998.

Nakanaela, Thomas K. *Ka Buke Moolelo o Hon. Robert William Wilikoki*. Honolulu: KHP, 1890.

Nicolaisen, W. F. "Why Tell Stories?" *Fabula* 31 (1990).

Nogelmeier, Puakea. *Mai Paʻa i ka Leo, Historical Voices in Hawaiian Primary Materials, Looking Forward and Listening Back*. Honolulu: Bishop Museum Press, 2010.

Perreira, Hiapo. "He Haʻiʻōlelo Kuʻuna: Nā Hiʻohiʻona me nā Kiʻina Hoʻāla Hou i nā Kākāʻōlelo (Classical Hawaiian Speechmaking: Aspects and Revitalization of Hawaiian Oratory)." Diss. Ka Haka ʻUla o ka Lani Center for Hawaiian Studies, University of Hawaiʻi at Hilo, 2011.

Pukui, Mary Kawena, and Samuel H. Elbert. *Hawaiian Dictionary*, rev. ed. Honolulu: University of Hawaiʻi Press, 1986.

Pukui, Mary Kawena, Samuel H. Elbert and Esther T. Mookini. *Place Names of Hawaii*, revised edition. Honolulu: University of Hawaiʻi Press, 1986.

Rice, William Hyde. "He Moolelo no Pele a me Kona Kaikaina Hiiakaikapoliopele." *Hoku o Hawaii*, May 21–September 10, 1908.

Richmond, Victoria. "The Roundup, Map of the Week: Native American Nations." January 8, 2014. http://thislandpress.com/roundups/map-of-the-week-native -american-nations/.

Tuhiwai Smith, Linda. *Decolonizing Methodologies, Research and Indigenous Peoples*, 2nd ed. New York: Zed Books, 2012.

Warrior, Robert. *The People and the Word, Reading Native Nonfiction*. Minneapolis: University of Minnesota Press, 2005.

Young, G. Terry Kanalu. *Rethinking the Native Hawaiian Past*. New York: Garland, 1998.

5

MOʻOKŪʻAUHAU AND MANA

ʻUMI PERKINS

If theory is a kind of "lens" through which one views the world, it is vital in academic work to examine the lens itself. This is especially true in fields such as Hawaiian "Studies" and Hawaiian history. Because of its significance to Hawaiian and other Indigenous worldviews, "genealogy" is a method that shows promise. In this chapter, I compare two types of genealogical methods, which challenge each other in some ways and are symbiotic in others: moʻokūʻauhau and mana and a Nietzschean and Foucauldian genealogical method. Moʻokūʻauhau and mana emphasize continuity of ancestral or other lineages, while Nietzschean and Foucauldian genealogy look for ruptures in such continuity. In other ways, these methodologies are complementary.

My research focus has been on Hawaiian and comparative land tenure within the field of critical political science, and I draw examples from that focus. I have found comparative genealogical approaches, such as moʻokūʻauhau, Nietzschean and Foucauldian genealogy, useful in bridging ideas about land tenure across cultures. Genealogy is one of the concepts I have identified in the emerging body of Indigenous theoretical frameworks. This framework has five recurring components: 1) the concept of harmony or balance, which can be seen in the structure of Indigenous societies and could be described as dynamic equilibrium or pono; 2) the importance of place and history; 3) experience, practice, and process; 4) the holistic and collective nature of indigeneity; and 5) the cyclical and genealogical nature of time.[1] I will attempt to locate this body of theoretical concepts within a specifically Hawaiian context—one applicable to land.

In the context that I examine genealogy here, I link it to the emerging field of Indigenous Studies that utilizes diverse theories. Māori researcher Linda Tuhiwai Smith, for example, cites Edward Said's (1978) idea of the Orient as "Other." The assertion that research is a significant site of struggle is thus an acknowledgment of the centrality of Said's work. She goes on: "in this example, the Other has been constituted with a name . . . *indigenous peoples*" (Smith 1999, 2). Smith uses Said's notion of "otherness" in an explication of the creation of a hierarchy of humanity. Creating the "oriental" imposed a construct that became part of a hierarchy that allowed for control and varying treatment of different Indigenous groups. Smith locates herself in a specific position as an Indigenous researcher. Foucault's notion of discipline is applied as part of Smith's construction of the relations between Indigenous peoples and their oppressors. She views many Western practices, including research, as disciplining the colonized.

Smith cites Said's questions: "Who writes? For whom is the writing being done? In what circumstances?" She views these questions as providing the "ingredients for a politics of interpretation" (Smith, 1999, 37). Smith acknowledges her debts to Western theories that are positioned as critiques of the enlightenment theoretical narrative. She lists two major examples of this "better" theory: Marxism and Western feminism (1999, 43). Of the two, Feminism is viewed as the more radical critique because of its challenge to epistemology, despite continuing challenges by "women of colour" (Smith 1999, 43).

Strauss and Corbin define methodology as "a way of thinking about and studying social reality," and methods as "a set of procedures and techniques for gathering and analyzing data" (1998). It is important in research to employ methods that are appropriate to the topics and historical periods examined. Because studies (such as my own work on land tenure) span multiple time periods, a layered and selective methodology may be appropriate, combining positivist and post-positivist methods to the appropriate historical periods. While certain methods come into vogue and are applied to any topic, it is crucial to examine which method is, in fact, appropriate to the topic.[2] Donovan Preza's MA thesis (2010) on the Māhele and land dispossession, for example, made the point that post-positivist methods were distorting understandings of Hawaiian land tenure. It was entitled "The Empirical Strikes Back." In my own work, I examine the transition from "traditional" Hawaiian land tenure to capitalist, European American–modeled land tenure, and assert that theory must adapt to this transition.The historical periods include that of traditional Hawaiian land tenure, the transition to the modern/Western land tenure system, and the post-Māhele period. Types of theory applied in this case include positivist legal theory, genealogy, Indigenous and Hawaiian theory, and postcolonial theory.

Only Indigenous and Hawaiian understandings informed traditional Hawaiian land tenure. The transition period reflects Western legal/positivist understandings blended with Indigenous and Hawaiian theoretical understandings diminishing in prominence, but still present. In the "modern" period, all three theoretical methods are applicable, with legal and postcolonial prominent (the latter particularly in the twentieth century), and Indigenous and Hawaiian present but de-emphasized, for example, through vestige laws from the Hawaiian Kingdom that exist as common law of the State of Hawai'i. A genealogical approach was applied during the entire period.

As Baden-Powell noted, "a comparative study . . . will bring out one thing: there are certain common factors which have, at least within wide geographical or ethnical limits always been at work in the production of the tenures we actually see around us in the several provinces (1892, 95)." This positivist approach, stringing facts like flowers on a lei, can be complemented by the frameworks of post-positivist, including postcolonial theorists, Linda Tuhiwai Smith's decolonized methodology, and the work of other Hawaiian and Indigenous theorists such as Manulani Aluli Meyer and Lilikalā Kame'eleihiwa.

Linda Tuhiwai Smith (1999) proposes a move toward an Indigenous methodology, and the outlines of such a method can be discerned in her book *Decolonizing Methodologies*. These outlines include proposals for community research, in which Indigenous communities set norms for research conducted by and on them, tribal research, and twenty-five "Indigenous projects." These include "indigenizing" (Smith 1999, 146), which "draws upon the traditions . . . evolved over many thousands of years," "revitalizing" (148), which draws on her involvement with the Kohanga Reo movement, and "representing," a right she claims "indigenous people have struggled since colonization to exercise," the right to "represent ourselves" (150). In research, one can move through focusing sequentially on positivist, interpretive, neo-Marxist, and postmodern (postcolonial) approaches.

Mo'okū'auhau and Genealogy: Continuity and Rupture

Mykännen views what I call theoretical encounters as a partial, cross-cultural translation, noting, "in the province of political knowledge . . . two cultures . . . approach each other. Yet the translation [is] not completed, because the comparisons [are] established in two distinct conceptual systems (2003, 118)." Such an encounter can occur between disparate cultural views of the concept of genealogy. I show the ways in which a Kanaka Maoli genealogy, mo'okū'auhau, challenges, and then comes into conversation with Nietzschean and Foucauldian genealogy.

MO'OKŪ'AUHAU

Malo (1987, 18) shows a nearly Nietzschean openness to the origins of Hawai'i's land, although it is important to question the accuracy of the Emerson translation:

1. He mea kahaha loa no ka manao i ka lohe ana mai i na olelo a ke poe kahiko no ke kumu o ka aina ana ma Hawaii nei, he kuee ko lakou mau manao aole he like pu
2. Maloko o na mookuauhau a lakou e ike ai lakou i ka okoa ana o na manao o lakou kekahi me kekahi

Emerson (1897, 3) translates:

1. It is very surprising to hear how contradictory are the accounts given by the ancients of the origin of the land here in Hawaii.
2. It is in their genealogies that we shall see the disagreement in this regard.

This surprising comfort with the contingent nature of "origin," is one area of resonance between mo'okū'auhau/genealogy, but it does not diminish its importance for Kānaka Maoli. Emerson translates "okoa" ('oko'a) as "disagreement," but it could easily be rendered "another," evoking a sense of plurality in the multiple versions of mo'okū'auhau.[3] An alternate way of viewing the plural aspect of mo'okū'auhau is as competing narratives, each of which is in itself continuous. As Cachola-Abad (2000) notes, mo'okū'auhau are internally consistent and reliable as data. Thus, mo'okū'auhau can have renderings emphasizing both continuity and rupture. As mo'okū'auhau is central to Hawaiian identity, this has effects on Hawaiian identity politics.

Halualani asserts that Hawaiian identity in the twentieth and twenty-first centuries is closely tied to genealogy (mo'okū'auhau) and land, particularly claims for Hawaiian Home Lands:

As a result of the Hawaiian Homes Commission Act (HHCA), a Native Hawaiian means "any descendant of not less than one-half part of the blood of the races inhabiting the Hawaiian Islands previous to 1778." In order to claim Hawaiianess and homestead leases and benefits in the name of Hawaiians, individuals must formally substantiate their 50 percent blood quantum. . . . Many

Hawaiians to this day, however, cannot formally prove their
Hawaiianess. (2002, xiv)

Halualani also documents the perceived connection between Hawaiian ethnicity and residence in Hawai'i. Land is thus racialized and genealogy is
central to Hawaiian identity formation.

Noted genealogist Lilikalā Kame'eleihiwa holds that "genealogies are
perceived by Hawaiians as an unbroken chain that links those today to the
primeval forces—to the *mana* (spiritual power) that first emerged with the
beginning of the world. Genealogies anchor Hawaiians to our place in the
universe and give us the comforting illusion of continued existence" (1992,
19–20). She continues, noting in regard to the illusory nature of the connection, that historical accuracy is "less important than the received *mana* of
the names" (344).

It is with this acknowledgment of the role of power that mo'okū'auhau
and Nietzschean and Foucauldian genealogies come into resonance. Foucault
showed the central role of power—which he defines as "the multiplicity of
force relations immanent in the sphere in which they operate and which constitute their own organization" (1978)—in methodology. While Foucault's
analysis is applied to a modern context, its political nature and focus on the
"power" of the state and related institutions, is relevant to mo'okū'auhau and
mana. They are assertions of the same types of power that are concerned
with the right to rule. Both are thus appropriate methods for use in the field
of political science.

Noelani Goodyear-Ka'ōpua asserts that while "our mo'okū'auhau
are certainly powerful truth claims . . . [o]ur genealogies are not just pro-
nouncements. Uttering them creates space for discussion and debate"
(2005). Noting the many consequential events of the nineteenth century,
Kame'eleihiwa expands on the function of mo'okū'auhau, stating that "genealogies also brought Hawaiians comfort in times of acute distress" (1992,
20). She holds that genealogies offered "proof that the race still existed as a
great nation" in times when Western practices seemed to render them "irrel-
evant" (20). Finally, citing the significance of genealogies in political power,
Kame'eleihiwa notes that ali'i are "the totality of their genealogy, which is
comprised of the character of their ancestors. [Mo'okū'auhau] is the sum total
of their identity." Discussing Hawaiian historical figures without examining
their mo'okū'auhau, she posits, would be "unintelligible" (21).

Mo'okū'auhau, then, emphasizes continuity. In this sense, mo'okū'auhau
appears as the obverse of a Nietzschean/Foucauldian genealogy, which privi-
leges disparity. But this continuity is acknowledged to be an "illusion"—
mana, rather than lineage or continuity, constitutes the actual significance
of mo'okū'auhau. It is in this sense of the term, with its emphasis on power
that the two concepts begin to resonate. Nietzschean and Foucauldian

genealogies' emphasis on rupture approximates the narratives of the early moʻolelo, in which time has obscured continuity. In the later moʻolelo (in what archaeologists would call the "proto-historic" period), continuity is more established. Further, by emphasizing "blood" on the one hand and "biopolitics" on the other, both are embodied practices. There is another way in which moʻokūʻauhau and genealogy are compatible, namely that genealogy primarily critiques the scientific. Such a critique was not inconsistent with the approach of the philosopher Friedrich Nietzsche.

NIETZSCHE'S GENEALOGY

To understand the "source" of his genealogical method, Nietzsche (2006) reminisced on his method's hazy origin, which began with a deconstruction of the "English," upside-down genealogy and its invocation of "heritage." It aims to "replace the improbable with the more probable," recognizing that that which replaces "error" may be, in fact, more error. This portrays genealogy as uninterested, particularly in grand metanarratives of glorious origin; thus genealogy is "quotidian," commonplace, or as Nietzsche put it, "gray"—the color of "what is documented, what can actually be confirmed and has actually existed" (1989, 21). Finally, this founding document of the genealogical method notes its "constrained" nature, and allows, at least in this early manifestation, for "backsliding and vacillation."

What was so offensive about the "English" hypothesis regarding moral sentiments, as epitomized by the philosopher Paul Ree? As Small shows, Ree offered a Darwinian theory of morality coupled with the notion that "idealism was demonstrable without being intelligible" (2007, 160). He claimed that, "the ethical problem has been solved. We know why many actions seem praiseworthy to us, and others blameworthy"—namely because it is evolutionarily beneficial (Ree, quoted in Small 2007, 162). It was the idealist aspect of Ree's approach that Nietzsche objected to rather than the Darwinian. As he states in *Daybreak*, "Formerly one sought the feeling of grandeur of man by pointing to his divine *origin*: this has now become a forbidden way, for at its portal stands the ape, together with other gruesome beasts, grinning as if to say: no further in this direction!" (1997, 47). As Foucault noted, "Paul Ree was wrong to follow the English tendency in describing the history of morality in terms of a linear development" (1977, 139). Evolutionary theory erected a roadblock to such teleological methods and desires.

Foucault, who viewed genealogy as the proper method of historical inquiry, contends that historians had "the obstinate [habit of] 'placing of conclusions at the beginning,' of 'making last things first,'" a practice he derisively calls "Egyptianism" (1977, 156). This practice imposes an illustrious heritage on a culture's origin. Nietzsche and Foucault both seem to ask whether one's origin could not be, instead, ignominious. Genealogy thus rejects any teleological approach, and even the dialectical approach of a

Marxian historical materialism, preferring instead to allow history to unfold "warts" and all. As Foucault held, genealogy "rejects the meta-historical deployment of ideal significations and indefinite teleologies." Foucault contests the historian's faith in reason, and supports Nietzsche's critique of moral values assumed to be embedded in historical development:

> . . . if the genealogist refuses to extend his faith in metaphysics, if he listens to history, he finds that there is "something altogether different" behind things: not a timeless and essential secret, but the secret that they have no essence or that their essence was fabricated in a piecemeal fashion from alien forms. (1977, 142)

In his 1973 book, *I, Pierre Riviere, Having Slaughtered My Mother, My Sister, and My Brother: A Case of Parricide*, Foucault drew from multiple sources in a way that illustrates the genealogical method: medical and legal records, police testimony, and Riviere's remarkable memoir of the acts. As Foucault noted in the foreword to the book, it was "an affair, a case, an event that provided the intersection of discourses that differed in form and origin." Similarly, in my work on Hawaiian land tenure, I draw on legal documents from the Kingdom, Territory, and State, letters of actors in the Māhele process, policy papers, oli and mele, and oral histories, in addition to academic sources, to look at the intersection of disparate narratives and arrive at more profound understandings of processes and events.

Commonalities emerge from a comparison of moʻokūʻauhau, Nietzschean and Foucauldian genealogies; all are cognizant of disparity in lineal descent (I would argue both of ancestry and of ideas), and all are concerned with power (mana). In my research, I examine the politics of land in each of these three domains, as a subject of knowledge and as a moral object, and in relation to a field of power.

Malo exhibits a nearly Nietzschean detached impartiality in origin, as his examinations of early Hawaiian history show. Regarding the early peopling of Hawaiʻi, Malo relates:

> A mahope mai o Lailai ma, ua hai hou ia mai, am ka mookuauhau I kapa ia Ololo, he kane ia kanaka mua loa, o Kahiko knoa inoa, ua olelo ia mai no kona mau kupuna a mau makua, me ka maopopo ole, o ko kakou ano, Kahiko no kai maopopo mai he kanaka ia.

> After Laʻilaʻi and others, it was again stated in the genealogy called *Lolo* that the very first person was a male. Kahiko was his name. It was said that the nature or being of his ancestor was not known. It is known that Kahiko was a human. (2006, 4)

Malo continues:

> from Kapawa until today, people have been known to have been
> born in the Hawaiian Islands. It, however, has not been told if they
> came from ʻOlolomehani. It has not been told who the first were
> to arrived [*sic*] and settle in the Hawaiian Islands. It has not been
> told if they came on canoes, and it has not been told what time
> their voyage to the Hawaiian Islands took place. (Chun, trans.,
> 2006, 5)

Malo's disclaimer "it has not been told" runs contrary to the Catholic
Hawaiian scholar Kepelino's assertion of a grander origin in the story of
Hawaiʻiloa. Addressing the notable disparities between Kepelino's account
and those of other Hawaiian scholars, Arista notes that some "Hawaiians tried
to bridge the gap between the two traditions—Hawaiian and Christian—by
attempting confusion. The Hawaiian Roman Catholic Zepherino Kepelino
altered Hawaiian traditions so that they would better fit his new Christian
paradigms" (1998, 90, citing Beckwith 1932). There is, then, disparity within
and between Hawaiian sources on origin. Rather than viewing this as a
weakness, it can be seen as bringing moʻokūʻauhau and genealogy into closer
conversation.

Some of the discrepancies that emerge from the attempt to order
Hawaiian moʻolelo can be mitigated by considering them over time. Cachola-
Abad (2000) holds that the Hawaiian genealogical record is internally consistent and reliable as data, but she focuses on the twenty-three generations
between voyaging chiefs such as Maweke and Kamehameha I. Earlier than
this, genealogies are less consistent, as are creation moʻolelo pertaining to several relevant questions. These questions include those concerning the origin
of Hawaiians, dates of settlement, first humans (mortals and ākua—gods). If
Stannard (1989) is correct, there may have been as few as one hundred settlers in approximately 300 AD—not sufficient for any "glorious" origin, but
rather a situation of survival.

As Malo notes on the consistency of early and late moʻokūʻauhau:

> Aole i Akaka ka moolelo o na [a]lii kahiko, o na [a]lii mai a
> Kealiiwahine mai, a me Lailai kana wahine, a mai a Kahiko mai,
> a me Kupulanakehau [kehau] kana wahine, a ma ia Wakea mai
> a me Papa kana wahine, a hiki mai ia Liloa, aole I lohe pono ia
> ko lakou mau moolelo ua lohe iki ia nae kahi mau olelo o kekahi
> mau alii kahiko, aole lohe nui ia, a mai ka Liloa a mai, a hiki
> mai ia Kamehameha akahi, ua akaka iki paha ko lakou moolelo.
> (2006, 133)

The traditions of the ancient ali'i are not quite clear. . . . The [tra-
ditions of the] ali'i from the time of Keali'iwahine and La'ila'i, his
wife, and from Kahiko and his wife, Kupulanakehau, and from
Wākea and his wife, Papa to Lo'iloa have not been accurately
heard. Some statements ('ōlelo) have been particularly retained
[heard] about these ancient ali'i(s) but not a lot has been actually [retained or] heard of. [However,] the traditions, from the
time of Līloa until Kamehameha I, are well known. (Chun, trans.,
2006, 182)

Further, genealogy and mo'okū'auhau are compatible in one additional
sense. As Foucault noted, "it is really against the effects of a discourse that
is considered to be scientific that the genealogy must struggle" (1980). If
"scientific" is defined as that body of knowledge derived through the use of
the scientific method, then Hawaiian genealogies do not qualify, and gain a
measure of exemption from genealogy's cutting gaze. De Goede notes that
Nietzsche critiqued historical method not for being laden with a vestige of
religious belief, but rather for an *over-dependence* on science. By critiquing the hegemony of purportedly "scientific" methodologies, which demean
Hawaiian and Indigenous worldviews, we can claim the right to utilize and
develop empowering methods that retain the rigor and predictive power of
traditional approaches.

Concluding Thoughts: Hawaiian and Scientific

Hawaiian thought, while rightly described by some as scientific, at the same
time contests science. In Hawaiian thought, intuition is considered to be
a reliable source of truth, whereas the intellect is considered "a deceiver"
(Ka'imikaua, quoted in Minton 2000). Hō'ailona, or signs in the environment,
used for decision making, are not considered controversial. For example,
Kamehameha decided to go to battle if "the feather god Kūka'ilimoku encouraged him to fight, for its feathers bristled and stood upright" (Kamakau
1992, 148). What could be interpreted as the use of subtle, environmental
cues is, in Hawaiian thought, direct communication from nā ākua (gods).
That environmental cues are not a criterion that would be used by modern
Western leaders shows the significance of intuitive experience in Indigenous
and Hawaiian thought.

In contrast to such intuitive practices, and to its own professed faith
in reason, modern science and theory practice a systematic, and systemic,
dismissal of intuition. Sheldrake relates a story of one such dismissal in an
encounter by villagers in Maine, France, with a meteor, a phenomenon not
explicable by the prevailing laws of Newtonian physics:

Several villagers heard a noise like a thunderclap, followed by a whistling sound, and saw something falling into a meadow. It turned out to be a stone too hot to touch. A local priest sent part of it to the Academy of Sciences in Paris for identification. The chemist Lavoisier ground it up, did some tests, and claimed he had proved it had not fallen from the sky, but instead was an ordinary stone that had probably been struck by lightning. He told the academy, "There are no stones in the sky. Therefore stones cannot fall from the sky." (2003, 3–4)

In contrast to a genealogical, and even a scientific approach, such a logic puts theory before observation. Ranciere states that in the field of aesthetics the idea of modernity is a questionable notion. Modernity in general, and science in particular, emerge as belief systems as much as rational practices. Hawaiian practices such as mo'okū'auhau can confront modernist belief systems in concert with genealogy.

One further area of contact between mo'okū'auhau and genealogy is in the notion of subjectivity. As Michael Clifford notes:

Following Foucault, the guiding methodological question [of a genealogical approach] is not, "What is the political subject?" but rather, "How are political subjects formed?" The first question is metaphysical; that is, it inquires into the essence of political subjectivity. The second question, on the other hand, is *genealogical*; it inquires into the contingent historical, discursive and non-discursive conditions of the emergence of political subjects. (2001, 6)

Summarizing Foucault's transition from archaeology to genealogy, Clifford notes that the latter method "sheds light on given historically contingent events, without pretense that they refer to foundational or universal structures that govern the formation of human thought or practice" (2001, 20). One purpose of genealogy, as Clifford describes it, is to disclose the constitution, or formation of the subject and then "get rid" of it, in order to recapture the historical processes leading to its formation:

Foucault is concerned with the limits that circumscribe human beings so as to transform them into *subjects*: medical subjects, sexual subjects, incarcerated subjects, [or sovereign subjects] and so on. "My objective," says Foucault, "has been to create a history of the different modes by which, in our culture, human beings are made subjects." (2001, 21)

Foucault holds one must then abolish the subject as a construction that blocks the full realization of a genealogical history.

This is one of the ways in which genealogy and moʻokūʻauhau can be brought into conversation with one another and be rendered into two "gazes" through which to perceive the creation of Hawaiian subjects, and developments in Hawaiian land tenure. As Kauanui notes, whose work focuses on the legal production of Hawaiian identity, the genealogical method "is embedded in indigenous epistemologies whereby peoplehood is rooted in the land" (2008, 10). This notion of the connectedness of "peoplehood" and land was directly confronted by the introduction of Western norms surrounding land. This confrontation constitutes what I call *theoretical encounter*. Moʻokūʻauhau is an appropriate methodology for the study of theoretical encounter as it apprehends the play of power/mana at the juncture where ideas and culturally embedded understandings meet.

Notes

1. See 'Umi Perkins, "Pono and the *Koru*: Indigenous Theory in Pacific Island Literature," *Hulili: Multidisciplinary Research in Hawaiian Well-Being* 4, no. 1 (2007).
2. Donovan Preza's MA thesis (2010) on the Māhele and land dispossession, for example, made the point that post-positivist methods were distorting understandings of Hawaiian land tenure. It was entitled "The Empirical Strikes Back."
3. wehewehe.org provides the following definitions for ʻokoʻa: "Different, separate, unrelated, another; whole; entirety; a whole note in music; entirely, wholly, completely; altogether, fully, independently, exclusively."

References

Arista, Denise Noelani Manuela. 1998. "Davida Malo, ke Kanaka o ka Huliau—David Malo, a Hawaiian of the Time of Change." MA thesis, religion, University of Hawaiʻi, Mānoa.

Baden-Powell, Baden Henry. 1892. *Land Systems of British India*, vol. 1. Oxford: Clarendon Press.

Beckwith, Martha. 1970. *Hawaiian Mythology*. Honolulu: University of Hawaiʻi Press.

Cachola-Abad, Kēhaunani. 2000. "The Evolution of Hawaiian Socio-political Complexity." Unpublished diss., University of Hawaiʻi, Mānoa.

Clifford, Michael. 2001. *Political Genealogy after Foucault: Savage Identities*. London: Routledge.

De Goede, Marieke. 2005. *Virtue, Fortune, and Faith: A Genealogy of Finance*. Minneapolis: University of Minnesota Press.

Foucault, Michel. 1984. *The Foucault Reader*, edited by P. Rabinow. New York: Pantheon Books.

———. 1978. *The History of Sexuality*, vol. 1: *An Introduction*. New York: Vintage Books.

———, ed. 1975. *I, Pierre Riviere, Having Slaughtered My Mother, My Sister, and My Brother: A Case of Parricide*. Lincoln: University of Nebraska Press.

———. 1977. *Language, Counter-memory, Practice: Selected Essays and Interviews*. Ithaca, NY: Cornell University Press.

Goodyear-Kaʻōpua, Jennifer Noelani. 2005. "Ku i ka mana: Building Community and Nation through Contemporary Hawaiian Schooling." Doctoral dissertation. Retreived from ProQuest.

Halualani, Rona. 2002. *In the Name of Hawaiians: Native Identities and Cultural Politics*. Minneapolis: University of Minnesota Press.

Kamakau, Samuel Mānaiakalani. 1992. *Ruling Chiefs of Hawaiʻi*. Honolulu: Kamehameha Schools Press.

Kameʻeleihiwa, Lilikalā. 1992. *Native Land and Foreign Desires: Pehea Lā e Pono Ai?* Honolulu: Bishop Museum Press.

Kauanui, J. Kēhaulani. 2008. *Hawaiian Blood: Colonialism and the Politics of Sovereignty and Indigeneity*. Durham, NC: Duke University Press.

Malo, David. 1987. *Hawaiian Antiquities*, translated by N. Emerson. Honolulu: Bishop Museum Press.

———. 2006. *Ka mooolelo Hawaii*, translated by M. N. Chun. Honolulu: First People's Productions.

Meyer, Manulani Aluli. 2004. *Hoʻoulu: Our Time of Becoming: Collected Early Writings of Manulani Meyer*. Honolulu: ʻAi Pohaku Press.

Minton, Nālani. 1992. *A Mau a Mau*. Honolulu: Na Maka o ka Aina.

Mykkänen, Juri. 2003. *Inventing Politics: A New Political Anthropology of the Hawaiian Kingdom*. Honolulu: University of Hawaiʻi Press.

Nietzsche, Friedrich. 1997. *Daybreak: Thoughts on the Prejudices of Morality*, edited by M. Clark and B. Leiter. Cambridge: Cambridge University Press.

———. 2006. *On the Genealogy of Morality*. Cambridge: Cambridge University Press.

Perkins, ʻUmi. 2007. "Pono and the *Koru*: Indigenous Theory in Pacific Island Literature." *Hūlili: Multidisciplinary Research on Hawaiian Well-Being* 4, no. 1.

Ranciere, Jacques. 2004. *The Politics of Aesthetics*. London: Continuum.

Said, Edward. 1978. *Orientalism*. New York: Vintage Books.

Sheldrake, Rupert. 2003. *The Sense of Being Stared At: And Other Unexplained Powers of Human Minds*. New York: Crown Publishers.

Small, Robin. 2007. *Nietzsche and Rée: A Star Friendship*. Oxford: Oxford University Press.

Smith, Linda Tuhiwai. 1999. *Decolonizing Methodologies: Research and Indigenous Peoples*. London: Zed Books.

Stannard, David. 1989. *Before the Horror: The Population of Hawaiʻi on the Eve of Western Contact*. Honolulu: Social Science Research Institute, University of Hawaiʻi.

Strauss, Anselm, and Juliet Corbin. 1998. *Basics of Qualitative Research: Techniques and Procedures for Developing Grounded Theory*. London: Sage Publications.

6

FROM MALIHINI TO HOAʻĀINA

Reconnecting People, Places, and Practices

HŌKŪLANI K. AIKAU

I should have known better but I didn't. I let myself get caught up in the thrill of the invitation of being asked to work with Kākoʻo ʻŌiwi, a Native Hawaiian nonprofit working to restore loʻi kalo (wetland taro farming) in the ahupuaʻa of Heʻeʻia[1] on Oʻahu Island, that I accepted without fully understanding the who, what, where, and why of it all. I said "yes" and never looked back. I agreed to join the research team because of the opportunity it afforded for doing community participatory research. I was eager to join a project committed to making the ʻāina (land, that which feeds) momona (abundant) once again. Early on in the project it was very clear that my positionality as a diasporic Hawaiian would be a problem for some members of the larger community. Although I knew I would need to build trust, I failed to fully grasp the degree to which I would be considered malihini (a stranger, foreigner). I structure this chapter around three ethnographic moʻolelo (vignettes) in order to think through the challenges of doing ethnographic research with a community to whom I am not genealogically connected. These moʻolelo also allow me to think deeply about the terms Native, non-Native, settler, and malihini in the context of land-based Indigenous research. My goal is to open up a critical dialogue about how each of us must interrogate our material, not just metaphorical, relationships with places if we are to take seriously kanaka ways of thinking, doing, and being in relation to ʻāina. I offer the concept of hoaʻāina (a friend of the land) as a way to be attentive to individual relationships to ʻāina that are not reckoned by moʻokūʻauhau but are forged by working with and for the land.

Moʻolelo ʻEkahi, "I got this"

> *May 2009: I meet with Kanekoa Shultz and Flo Thomas at Starbucks in Kāneʻohe so they can give me background on the loʻi restoration project and then Koa will take me to the farm for a tour. I am new to the project having been invited to join the re-search team just a few weeks earlier. Koa gives me a brief history of the site where the restoration is taking place, background on how the community resistance to development was instrumental in preventing this area from turning into another Hawaiʻi Kai,[2] and that the project is being pushed forward by kūpuna (elders) active in the Koʻolauoko Hawaiian Civic Club. Koa warns me that as a Hawaiian, the kūpuna will have different expectations of me than they will of Flo [who is not Hawaiian]. I tell him that I understand and that I fully expected as much. The meeting continues for another fifteen minutes, then Koa takes me to the farm. Several months later, I hear from Koa that some kūpuna question my role on the research team because I am not from the moku (district) or ahupuaʻa (smaller land division). He assures me not to worry about it. A seed of worry is planted.*

This meeting took place about eighteen months before I began actively working with Kākoʻo ʻŌiwi. The name of the project is Māhuahua ʻAi o Hoi, the restoration of food/poi in Hoi, the ili (smaller land division within the ʻahupuaʻa) where the first loʻi was restored after forty years of being filled in with topsoil and left fallow. As this opening scene illustrates, I began this project confident in my role as the Kanaka ʻŌiwi (Native Hawaiian) researcher on the team. I was very aware that my kuleana (roles and responsibilities) would be different from my haole (non–Native Hawaiian) colleagues, and that as a Kanaka ʻŌiwi we all assumed I had an "insider" perspective that we hoped would help move the project forward. In retrospect, my confidence was a product of academic hubris, a false confidence based on an intellectual understanding, not an embodied, relational one. Indeed, I truly felt prepared to accept the invitation and felt cautiously confident about my positionality. After all, the insider/outsider dilemma (Smith 2012; Tengan 2005, 2008; Tengan, Kaʻili, and Fonoti 2010; Collins 2008) and critical positionality

(Haraway 1991; Nielsen and Gould 2007) are central themes in my research methods courses at both the undergraduate and graduate levels. Given my previous research working with my own community I felt confident that I could manage my insider/outsider status in this new context (Aikau 2010, 2012).

I realize I was naive and I should have been more prepared for what was to come next. Fast-forward several months to the first team meeting with the "aunties" (the group of mostly women who were the visionaries and drivers of the project). I had prepared an introduction that I thought would show the aunties that I had something useful to offer. At the opening of the meeting, we went around the room and introduced ourselves. Each of us presented our moʻokūʻauhau (genealogy) as it related to the project. I shared my Hawaiian familial lineage by introducing my father, Ned Aikau, whose family comes from Hana, Maui, and Kohala, Hawaiʻi. I talked about my tūtūwahine (grandmother), Keala Kaʻaihue, who was from Molokaʻi but raised on Maui by her tūtū wahine who taught her how to grow kalo. I also acknowledged that I was not raised in Hawaiʻi but grew up in Utah on the territories of the Navajo, Shoshone, and Ute Nations. I stressed that I was returning "home" after having been away thirty years. I explained my role as a social scientist on the team and shared my personal reasons for wanting to be part of the project: I was eager to be part of a process that would allow me to reconnect with ʻāina while also working to help the ʻāina become momona again.

They responded with suspicion. I was unprepared for this reaction and I was hurt. Although I did not expect them to welcome me immediately, that I would need to earn their trust, I did expect a certain level of puʻuwai aloha (generosity) from them since I was willing to step up to do the work. What I did not expect was the dismissive way they responded to my introduction. Although I have worked hard to be dependable and trustworthy, some of the aunties are still suspicious. It was not until later that I came to see the situation from their point of view. For not unlike the ʻōlelo noʻeau (poetical saying) that reads "No nehinei aʻe nei no; he aha ka ʻike?"—This person just arrived, what do they know?—I was a stranger to this place, both Heʻeʻia and in many ways to Hawaiʻi, and I had much to learn.

In this chapter I take up a particular puzzle relating to positionality. At the core of this puzzle is a question: who is a Native and a stranger to a place and what kuleana comes with this status? I provisionally interpret kuleana to mean roles, responsibility, and obligations, but as I discuss below kuleana is a much more complex term than this gloss allows. Through moʻokūʻauhau or genealogy kuleana connects people, ʻāina, ancestors, and actions in a cooperative, relational set of obligations that a person accepts and willingly carries through their lifetime. This essay seeks to flesh out in physical and material ways how kuleana is both a set of ethical principles and material practices that fundamentally re-form and in-form our human and other-than-human relationships in places. These moʻolelo map how my journey of transformation working with ʻāina and mahiʻai kalo (taro farmers) has fundamentally shifted my understanding of the insider/outsider dilemma in research and are an invitation to other malihini to pursue a path for becoming hoa with ʻāina. I use the ethnographic research I have done with Kākoʻo ʻŌiwi to assert that the process of re/establishing a connection to ʻāina is not only important for Indigenous people, I firmly believe that it is critical to the health and well-being of Indigenous nations that we in fact re-form our relationships to our ancestors, territories, and the knowledge that lives in these people and places. But I am also deeply committed to thinking about how to re-orient non-Natives to ʻāina so that they too can ethically participate in an Indigenous future that supports all of us.

When I began this project I was perfectly comfortable framing this puzzle using the Native/non-Native binary. It was a framework that seemed to make sense. Indeed, settler colonialism as a theoretical framework utilizes such a binary in order to make visible Indigenous claims to land and sovereignty (Trask 2008), while also explaining how it functions as a system of policies and practices intent on the elimination of those same Indigenous claims and the people who make them (Wolfe 2006). Settler colonialism as a structure is fundamentally intent on claiming and controlling land and labor—it is about dispossession and accumulation through the elimination of the Native. It is an effective theoretical framework for understanding the political, rhetorical, and discursive fields of past and present Indigenous movements. But settler colonialism does not have a vision for an Indigenous futurity; the future it imagines and plans for (and that we can critique) is a settler futurity and this is not acceptable. Additionally, when looking methodologically on the ground it appears to be far too simple a framework because it cannot grapple with the Indigenous frameworks that precede and exceed the settler colonial state apparatus. Settler colonialism can only explain, in broad theoretical strokes, the systems and structures of power as they are and why they came to be. It is not a theoretical framework that can explain how to transform the system or to envision an Indigenous futurity. A different framework is needed if we are to imagine and plan for an alternative, Indigenous future. For this I turn to Indigenous resurgence as the methodological and theoretical framework I rely upon in order to move from why to how.

Whereas settler colonialism explains how Indigenous peoples became disconnected from our lands, language, histories, and ceremonial cycles, Indigenous resurgence seeks to revive and fortify these connections while also seeking to restore Indigenous responsibilities and respect for one another, land, and culture through everyday acts of resurgence. For several years now I have been interested in those everyday acts of resurgence that reconnect Kanaka ʻŌiwi Hawaiʻi to our land- and water-based practices.

Unlike Indigenous rights' approaches that focus on Indigenous–State inter-action through policy, programs, and interventions intended to increase ca-pacity and build resilience (the underlying assumption being that Indigenous peoples lack both and thus need the hetero-paternalism of the state and its surrogates to restore them), Indigenous resurgence focuses on those things that restore a sense of individual and communal responsibility for our lan-guage, histories, territories, ceremonial cycles, and intellectual practices (Alfred and Corntassel 2005). For Anishnabe scholar and poet, Leanne Simpson, Indigenous resurgence begins with each individual seeking out the wisdom that lives in the stories left to us by our ancestors and figuring out how those messages can guide our actions today for the benefit of future generations. This is not a process that can be prescribed but is the responsibil-ity of each person to find meaning in the stories and to take action. Simpson has a very clear directive for how we do this. She writes, "the process of re-surgence must be Indigenous at its core in order to reclaim and re-politicize the context and the nature of Nishnaabeg thought" (2011, 20). The moʻolelo I share in this essay tell a larger story about how I had to shift my thinking about the insider/outsider dilemma if I was going to engage in this project in a truly Hawaiian-centered way.

I also want to acknowledge in advance that the place I want to take this discussion may be dangerous as I am not sure what the larger political implications of my analysis might be, as I take up and interrogate the sub-ject position of the Native and ask how do we hold each other accountable for our actions? Who is kamaʻaina (a child of the land) and who is mali-hini (a stranger) to a place? How and why do these categories matter in an Indigenous resurgent framework? The personal question for me in relation-ship to this work is, how does a child of the Hawaiian diaspora return to and reconnect with ʻāina? How do I do this when the ʻāina I am working with is not my one hānau (birth sands/the birthplace of my ancestor) or ke kula iwi (the plains where our bones are buried)? I do not have all the answers to these questions, but I am interested in thinking through the relationship between what we do (the theoretical and political frameworks we operate within) and how we put them into practice. To be sure, at the core of Indigenous re-surgence is re-establishing and re-enforcing the relationship among people, places, and practices.

Moʻolelo ʻElua, "Who me, mahaʻoi?"

On my way into campus, I stop at Longs Drugs to pick up something I need for a trip. I am getting ready to leave for a conference where I will give a presentation on my new research project. I run into a Kanaka ʻŌiwi colleague whom I have not seen for a while. She asks how I am doing and what I am up to. I tell her about the conference

so she asks about my paper. I tell her it is on my new research proj-
ect working with Kākoʻo ʻŌiwi in Heʻeʻia. In what I interpret to be
an abrasive tone, she asks why I am working in Heʻeʻia where I have
no kuleana. She asks, rhetorically, if it is mahaʻoi (intrusive) of me
to work there. In what she probably interpreted as a defensive tone,
I reply that I do not consider it mahaʻoi since I was invited to work
there. I did not initiate the invitation but accepted it when it came.
I leave the interaction feeling insecure. The seed of doubt in my
naʻau (gut) grows bigger. What is my kuleana?

My first response to my friend was to be defensive and put-off. But the more I
thought about my kuleana (my responsibilities and the limits of my authority
to make decisions relating to ʻāina for which I have no moʻokūʻauhau connection), the more I realized she might be right and that scared me. I began
by critically questioning everything I thought I knew about the insider/out-
sider binary. The feminist, critical ethnographic, and Indigenous research
literature describes the insider/outsider dilemma as a problem between
our—Indigenous, feminist, of color—roles as both researcher and community member and the often-competing commitments and demands of these
two positionalities. I realized that I needed to clear space between the Native/
non-Native binary and the insider/outsider positionality if I was going have a
productive dialogue about the various roles people, differentially positioned
in relationship to this project, can and should play in the restoration of loʻi
kalo. How does the Native/non-Native binary create other kinds of moves
to innocence, ones that do not necessarily reflect our Indigenous ontologies
but the limited optics required of colonization?[3] What appeared to be miss-
ing from the academy/community binary was a third dimension, genealogy
or moʻokūʻauhau. Moʻokūʻauhau is understood to be a way to map familial
and larger social relations as they exist in the place where we dwell, work, or
stand. As my colleagues and I have written elsewhere, kuleana is very much
connected to moʻokūʻauhau and must fundamentally inform how we do our
work (Aikau, Goodyear-Kaʻōpua, and Silva 2016). What does this web of relations oblige each of us to do in a particular place and time?
　　The encounter with my colleague pushed me to critically interrogate
my actual relationship to place, not a metaphorical one or one based on the
abstract category of Native Hawaiian. Rather, in order to strive to *not* be
mahaʻoi or intrusive I needed to acknowledge that I am malihini (not of a
place) and I needed to be okay with it. For although "ua hoʻi hou i ka iwi
kuamoʻo" I had returned to the land of my ancestors (Pukui 1983, 109), in
a general sense, I am not "ke ēwe hānau o ka ʻāina," I was not born of the
lineage of Heʻeʻia (Pukui 1983, 182). I did not have the kind of kuleana that
comes from moʻokūʻauhau, and to rely only on the generalized categories of
Native/non-Native was a move to innocence. It allowed me to sidestep my

actual, or lack thereof, relationships in, to, and with Heʻeʻia, and in the process I gave myself kuleana that was not earned and certainly not recognized by the kūpuna. I had to see myself through the eyes of the aunties and my colleague and admit that I was in fact being mahaʻoi.

My story could end there but it did not because I felt in my naʻau that I needed to be working at the loʻi for personal and professional reasons. Although I firmly acknowledge, respect, and prioritize the kuleana that comes from having a moʻokūʻauhau relationship to ʻāina, my work at the loʻi suggested that kuleana can take other forms; as one's relationship with ʻāina changed so could one's kuleana. To figure out this part of the puzzle, I turned to the words of my ancestors. There is an ʻōlelo noʻeau that aptly describes the role of the malihini in Hawaiian culture. "Hoʻokahi no lā o ka malihini" tells us that you can only be a stranger for a day and then you must contribute (Pukui 1983, 115). This ʻōlelo noʻeau reminded me that kuleana is not only about moʻokūʻauhau, it is also about being willing to work. I began to shift my thinking away from wanting to become kamaʻāina or kupaʻāina (a child of the land), to consider alternative relationships that can be forged with ʻāina that are not mahaʻoi but that can carry kuleana. I started to consider other terms that might better explain the kind of kuleana a malihini might establish at the loʻi.

I offer hoaʻāina as one possibility. The concept of hoaʻāina can be interpreted as a friend, caretaker, partner who is tied to and bound to ʻāina based on kuleana that is not genealogical but that comes from hanalima, working with our hands in the lepo (dirt, soil). ʻŌiwi scholar Kamana Beamer explains that in the nineteenth century hoaʻāina was the term for Native subjects of the Kingdom (2014). If we stretch the meaning of Native subjects from one related to citizenship and consider the ʻāina to be the source of ea (sovereignty and breath of life) then we can understand hoaʻāina to also mean subjects of the ʻāina, those who sustain the ea of the ʻāina. ʻŌiwi scholar Noelani Goodyear-Kaʻōpua interprets ea in this way:

> Ea can be seen as both a concept and a diverse set of practices. . . .
> Ea refers to political independence and is often translated as "sovereignty." It also carries the meaning of "life" and "breath," among other things. . . . Ea is based on the experiences of people on the land, relationships forged through the process of remembering and caring for wahi pana, storied places. . . . Ea is an active state of being. . . . Ea cannot be achieved or possessed; it requires constant action day after day, generation after generation.
> (Goodyear-Kaʻōpua, Hussey, and Wright 2014, 3–4)

Through the notion of ea we can see how hoaʻāina kuleana can emerge from working with and for the land. Handy and Pukui note that a mahiʻai kalo's (taro farmer's) ability to secure access to water and to increase the number of loʻi they are able to cultivate depended on the amount of labor they contributed to the building and maintaining of ʻauwai and to maintaining their existing loʻi. Mahiʻai kalo who could get large numbers of friends and family to help them with their work would be rewarded with greater amounts of resources—water and loʻi. In return, the friends and family were gifted with meaʻai (food) (Handy and Pukui 1972). When we increase our labor capacity we also increase our kuleana.

In a practical sense, I needed to figure out what to do to be hoaʻāina to Heʻeʻia; I needed to stop being a stranger and get to work. I opened my eyes, sharpened my listening skills, turned my hands down, and kept my mouth shut. I spent the first year "in the field" just watching, listening, and working. I did not do any formal "research," I just worked. The more I worked the more familiar the ʻāina became to me and, I think, me to it. It was a combination of one year of hanalima and then another two years doing participant observations and surveys that I was able to peel back another layer of meaning of hoaʻāina and started to see the orientations as critical to this new formation.

From our observations, fieldnotes, and the data we gathered from volunteer surveys we came to realize that volunteers make connections between Hawaiian culture, the environment, and local food issues during the orientations. My personal reflections confirmed that it was during orientations that I learned place-names, the names of ākua, and the moʻolelo about Heʻeʻia. One critical component of the Mahuahua ʻAi o Hoi project is to engage volunteers in a meaningful experience so they will "buy-into" the project and return to the loʻi every month for regularly scheduled workdays. At any given time Kākoʻo ʻŌiwi can only afford to pay three to six full-time employees who are responsible for maintaining two acres of loʻi and another acre of organic gardens. They rely heavily on volunteers to complete large tasks such as clearing fields and preparing loʻi for planting.

When I began attending community workdays, two staff members conducted the orientations: Kanekoa Kukea-Shultz, the executive director, provides volunteers with a history of the project and the environmental benefits of the restoration, and Kelsey, we will call her, wants volunteers to experience the loʻi as she experienced it everyday as a fundamentally Hawaiian place that when restored will bring native plants, animals, and Kanaka ʻŌiwi back to the land. Her approach was intended to help volunteers make an emotional and cultural connection to place.

Kelsey begins her portion of the introduction at the pond. Before we begin the five-minute walk to the loʻi, Kelsey directs our attention to the hao trees obscured by mangrove trees and introduces us to Meheanu, the moʻo (a reptilian, shape-shifting deity) and guardian of the fresh water in the wetland who lives under the hao trees barely visible beside the mangrove trees. Kelsey asks us to remember and acknowledge Meheanu when we come to the loʻi because this is her home and we are her guests.

Kelsey then draws our attention to two very distinct-looking plants and identifies them as the neke and the ʻakaʻakai, two native plants that have survived despite the changes in the ʻāina. She hopes that as volunteers help to restore loʻi more native plants and animals will be able to grow in the pond again. From the pond, she asks the group to follow her to the loʻi. When we are about halfway there, we stop and Kelsey directs our attention toward a particularly sharp and jagged ridgeline on the Koʻolau Mountains. She tells us that the ridge is a border that divides this ahupuaʻa from the next one. She tells us its name is ʻIolekaʻa, named after the ʻEwa rats that rolled down the hill. As the story goes, the ʻEwa rats would regularly sneak over the mountains to Heʻeʻia and steal the ono kalo they grew in abundance. But the Heʻeʻia rats got tired of the ʻEwa rats stealing their ʻai so they came up with a plan. They went to ʻEwa and invited the ʻEwa rats to come and enjoy their mea ʻai (food). The ʻEwa rats were very excited to eat the ono food from Heʻeʻia so they immediately followed the Heʻeʻia rats over the Koʻolau Mountains to the windward side. As they were traversing the narrow ridgeline the Heʻeʻia rats told the ʻEwa rats to be careful, but the ʻEwa rats never listen and with one wrong step all of the ʻEwa rats slipped off the ridge and rolled down the mountain. Kelsey ends by merely saying, "so that is the story of why that ridge is called Iolekaʻa." I look around at the group and folks take another moment to look at the ridge. I wonder what they must be thinking. For me the story is filled with lessons. The most important one for me is the reminder that we must not take the resources from other loʻi but should be invited to the loʻi where we should work to help grow the kalo we love.

Kelsey moves us forward again. The next stop is at the loʻi. She halts the group near loʻi #1 and explains that this was the first loʻi opened up by community members who saw the possibilities of what could be, spending weekends and evenings removing the tall grass, digging out the space, and carving out an ʻauwai to bring water to the kalo. In 2009, the first kalo was planted and since then they have opened up six more loʻi on approximately two acres of land. She explains that no machinery was used to open these loʻi, rather it was the hard work of volunteers like themselves who used shovels, picks, and brute strength to open these first taro patches.

Our final moʻolelo before we divide into different work crews is about the cultural significance of kalo. As the group looks out over the loʻi planted with kalo, Kelsey tells us the story of Hāloa. Within a Hawaiian worldview, Kalo is the kino lau (the plant form) of the first human child born of Wākea (the akua of the sky) and Hoʻohōkūkalani (the akua of the stars), named Hāloanākalaukapalili whose lifeless body was buried beside their hale and where grew the first kalo plant. Their second child, also a human and also a boy named Hāloa, lived to become a great aliʻi (chief, leader) of the Hawaiian people. From this story we learn that kalo is the elder sibling of Kanaka ʻŌiwi. We also learn that in his plant form, he will feed us if we mālama (care for and nurture) him. I know from my interview with Kelsey that this is the most important thing she wants volunteers to remember. She says,

> The Hāloa story . . . I always tell them, even if you forget every-thing I say today, don't forget this, cause that's the thing that shows you the link between [the] Hawaiian people, and the land, and the water, and the kalo. And I mean, I guess you can tell when people get that, because when you share that story there are always a handful of people who are like, "wow, so that's it."

For Kelsey, Hawaiian culture is the foundation of the work that they do and it is important to her that volunteers make these connections as well. Through her guided tour, Kelsey presents a new way of thinking about volunteerism not as work but as a form of cultivating a relationship with ʻāina.

Moʻolelo ʻEkolu, "He kalo a he kanaka"

In January 2012, I have my first taste of poi made from the kalo at Hoi. It tastes like the loʻi. I can feel the wind as it blows across the fields and see the lau dance, I can feel the sun on my skin, the humidity in the air, the sweat rolling like rivers down my face as we pull weeds, build puʻe, slather mud on the kūaona to reinforce it, to make it strong. I can taste the dark, slick, clayey mud that stains our clothes, gets caked under our nails. I smell the fecundity of the lepo, teeming with life. I sense the cool refreshing water that flows through the loʻi. Until that moment, I did not fully understand how kalo and kanaka are one.

My visceral response to eating ʻai that I had helped cultivate signaled a physi-ological shift in my being. The hanalima of that year changed me, brought me closer to ʻāina and helped me to understand things differently than I did before. Eating ʻai grown from the loʻi also signaled a shift in my relationship to the Kākoʻo staff with whom I have built trust. Today they feel comfort-able asking me to oversee volunteers on community workdays and they can rely on me to take on various projects in the loʻi and for research. They trust me enough to share their frustrations and struggles as well as include me in celebrations and talk stories. I still ask permission while at the loʻi because I have come to accept the limits of my kuleana as I gradually move from malihini to hoaʻāina.

I am reminded of Ty Kāwika Tengan's reflections in his essay "Unsettling Ethnography" that critical ethnography has the potential to disrupt "taken-for-granted understandings [making] it an especially useful tool for critiquing all ethnographic sites and participants" (2005, 248). This essay and my shifting standpoint in relationship to my research with Heʻeʻia reveal how important it is to disrupt and open up the binary between the Native/non-Native and the insider/outsider. I agree that critical ethnographic research is a productive way to interrogate our relationships to one another while working to restore our connections to ʻāina and the wisdom that lives in places. As Tengan goes on to explain,

> For anthropologists who claim a native identity, as well as others who collaborate as allies with indigenous causes, [the insider/outsider tension] may be felt more keenly because of the multiplicity of obligations, responsibilities and audiences they are held accountable to, especially given the stakes riding upon their work (Field 1999; Jacobs-Huey 2002). These issues have become increasingly important for all ethnographers to reckon with, as distinctions between insider/outsider, home/away and engaged/disengaged have become difficult to maintain, especially in the Pacific. (247)

This research has aided me in learning to become hoaʻāina. I do not think I have arrived at a destination, as I do not think there is a state of being "hoaʻāina" at which one arrives. Rather, it is an ongoing process of learning from and giving back to the ʻāina.

Notes

1. Heʻeia is more typically spelled without the diacritical marking between the e and i. I spell Heʻeʻia in this less common way in order to stress that heʻe references octopus (*Polypus sp.*) and also means to slide, surf, slip, or flee (Pukui 1983, 63). ʻIa is a particle marking the passive/imperative. In this phrasing, heʻe ʻia refers to the place abundant with heʻe and a place that is slippery from the abundant water in the ahupuaʻa.
2. Hawaiʻi Kai is a southern California–inspired subdivision developed in the 1950s during the post–World War II development boom on Oʻahu. Hawaiʻi Kai is located on the southeastern shores of Oʻahu, in the ahupuaʻa of Waimanalo, the ili of Maunalua.
3. The phrase "moves to innocence" is borrowed from Eve Tuck and K. Wayne Yang who describe those settler evasions and actions that attempt to address and redress settler guilt and complicity for colonization even as these very same moves produce and reproduce a settler futurity that necessitates the elimination of the

Native, the reproduction of white racial supremacy, and structures of heternormativity (Tuck and Yang 2012). My thinking about moves to innocence is also informed by the work of Jennifer L. Pierce whose ethnography of white male lawyers demonstrates how race and gender privilege are a blind spot in their everyday lives even as their daily actions work to reproduce such privilege. In doing so, they plead innocent to reproducing the systems and structures of privilege to which they are the benficiaries (Pierce 2012). In my usage of the phrase, I intend it as an opportunity for Indigenous studies scholars, differentially positioned in relationship to Indigenous communities and lands to critically reflect on our kuleana in order not to race for or move to innocence but to be ever dilligent about the obligations we have to ʻāina and the limits of our authority.

References

Aikau, Hokulani. 2010. "Indigeneity in the Diaspora: The Case of Native Hawaiians at Iosepa, Utah." *American Quarterly* 62, no. 3:477–500.

Aikau, Hokulani K. 2012. *A Chosen People, a Promised Land: Mormonism and Race in Hawaiʻi*. Minneapolis: University of Minnesota Press.

Aikau, Hokulani K., Noelani Goodyear-Kaʻōpua, and Noenoe K. Silva. 2016. "The Practice of Kuleana: Reflections on Critical Indigenous Studies through Trans-Indigenous Exchange." In *Critical Indigenous Studies: Engagements in First World Locations*, edited by Aileen Moreton-Robinson. Critical Issues in Indigenous Studies. Tucson: University of Arizona Press.

Alfred, Taiaiake, and Jeff Corntassel. 2005. "Being Indigenous: Resurgences against Contemporary Colonialism." *Government and Opposition* 40, issue 4:597–614.

Beamer, Kamanamaikalani. 2014. *No Makou Ka Mana: Liberating the Nation.* Honolulu: Kamehameha Publishing.

Collins, Patricia Hill. 2008. *Black Feminist Thought: Knowledge, Consciousness, and the Politics of Empowerment.* 1st ed. New York: Routledge.

Goodyear-Kaopua, Noelani, Ikaika Hussey, and Erin Kahunawaikaʻala Wright, eds. 2014. *A Nation Rising: Hawaiian Movements for Life, Land, and Sovereignty.* Durham, NC: Duke University Press.

Handy, Elizabeth Green, Edward Smith Craighill, and Mary Kawena Pukui. 1972. *Native Planters in Old Hawaii: Their Life, Lore, and Environment.* Honolulu: Bishop Museum Press.

Haraway, Donna. 1991. *Simians, Cyborgs, and Women: The Reinvention of Nature.* New York: Routledge.

Nielsen, Marianne O., and Larry A. Gould. 2007. "Non-Native Scholars Doing Resarch in Native American Communities: A Matter of Respect." *The Social Science Journal* 44:420–433.

Pierce, Jennifer. 2012. *Racing for Innocence: Whiteness, Gender, and the Backlash against Affirmative Action.* Stanford, CA: Stanford University Press.

Pukui, Mary Kawena. 1983. *ʻŌlelo Noʻeau: Hawaiian Proverbs and Poetical Sayings.* Honolulu: Bishop Museum Press.

Simpson, Leanne. 2011. *Dancing on Our Turtle's Back: Stories of Nishnaabeg Re-creation, Resurgence and a New Emergence.* Winnipeg: Arbeiter Ring Pub.

Smith, Linda Tuhiwai. 2012. *Decolonizing Methodologies: Research and Indigenous Peoples.* 2nd ed. London: Zed Books.

Tengan, Ty Kāwika. 2008. *Native Men Remade: Gender and Nation in Contemporary Hawai'i.* Durham, NC: Duke University Press.

———. 2005. "Unsettling Ethnography: Tales of an 'Ōiwi in the Anthropological Slot." *Anthropological Forum* 15, no. 3:247–256.

Tengan, Ty Kāwika, Tevita Ka'ili, and Rochelle Tuitagava'a Fonoti. 2010. "Genealogies: Articulating Indigenous Antrhopology in/of Oceania." *Pacific Studies* 33, no. 2/3:139–167.

Trask, Haunani-Kay. 2008. "Settlers of Color and 'Immigrant' Hegemony: 'Locals' in Hawai'i." In *Asian Settler Colonialism: From Local Governance to the Habits of Everday Life in Hawai'i,* edited by Candace Fujikane and Jonathan Y. Okamura, pp. 45–65. Honolulu: University of Hawai'i Press.

Tuck, Eve, and K. Wayne Yang. 2012. "Decolonization Is Not a Metaphor." *Decolonization: Indigeneity, Education & Society* 1 (1). http://decolonization.org /index.php/des/article/view/18630.

Wolfe, Patrick. 2006. "Settler Colonialism and the Elimination of the Native." *Journal of Genocide Research* 8, no. 4:387–409.

7

TRANSCENDING SETTLER COLONIAL BOUNDARIES WITH MOʻOKŪʻAUHAU

Genealogy as Transgressive Methodology

DAVID A. CHANG

Genealogical research can easily be dismissed as a self-absorbed and narrowing search for roots, but in my experience, exploring my own kūʻauhau (genealogy) brought central theoretical and methodological concerns to my attention: the ways that settler colonial categorization impedes our understanding of the Hawaiian past, and the power of moʻokūʻauhau to overcome those colonial constraints. American settler colonialism has naturalized a number of fictions to bolster its power. Two that frustrate the project of moʻokūʻauhau are the notion of the bounded, atomized individual and the concept of the firmly and stably bounded nation-state. Moʻokūʻauhau (genealogy), however, is a powerful practice that can help us to transgress (etymologically, to cross over) the lines that these restrictive fictions draw around us and our kūpuna. This essay contrasts moʻokūʻauhau with what I call the practice of "settler genealogy," a practice that reinforces claims for the legitimacy of settler power and the settler state via the tracing of biological lineage through heterosexual marriage bonds. At its best, moʻokūʻauhau rejects these limitations and traces the lines of Kanaka kinship in all its richness, providing us a means to understand ourselves, our ancestors, our relations, and those people who will be our descendants in broader contexts than we ever before imagined.

As a Kanaka Maoli who was raised in diaspora (specifically, Milwaukee in the 1970s and 1980s), I always yearned to study and learn more about my kūpuna and Hawai'i, but both always seemed distant and unknowable. My siblings and I knew that our grandfather and thus our father were Hawaiian and that our father was committed to that people and that identity. But our grandfather had passed away in the 1950s. He was an only child and his father was an only child. My father's generation had almost no contact with extended family on their father's side, the side on which their Kanaka Maoli ancestry lay. They knew little more than that they were of Hawaiian and Chinese descent. Learning more about his kū'auhau was hard, because like hundreds of other Kānaka of partly Chinese descent in the late nineteenth and early twentieth centuries, my grandfather was raised as a child in China by relatives there. He had little connection to his 'Ōiwi relations, even when he moved from China to Hawai'i in 1915 as a young man. This family history created two kinds of problems for learning more about my family's past. The first was a research problem: documents were scattered from Hawai'i to China to North America, and were in Hawaiian, Chinese, and English. A lack of access to documents and boundaries of language therefore made researching mo'okū'auhau difficult for me.

Another problem was more important still: colonial boundaries of social categorization that I had internalized. Boundaries of nationality, of authenticity, and of race that were taught to me by the society in which I grew up, place Hawaiian-speaking ancestors in South Kona, Hawai'i Island; Chinese-speaking ancestors in Ooshek village, China; and an English-speaking father in Milwaukee, Wisconsin, in altogether separate categories—not one coherent lineage, although all of these were descendants of the same Kanaka Maoli ancestors. My generation knew some of the names of our ancestors and some of the places they lived, but because I had internalized the boundaries of nation-states, especially settler nation-states, there seemed to be little meaningful relationship between those ancestors. I could see only disconnected individuals separated by national and racial boundaries.

It was only later, after training and research in Native American Studies, and after the emergence of an extraordinary generation of Kanaka Maoli scholars who opened new doors of understanding, that I could delve deeply into Hawaiian studies, Hawaiian language study, and simultaneously into the study of my kū'auhau. I began to see how the few facts I know about my ancestors were not unconnected names and places, but part of a mo'olelo: a *story*, a *history*. It was only by using Hawaiian language documents and Hawaiian Kingdom sources—everything from newspaper stories on the travels of people between China and Hawai'i to land records, birth records, marriage records, entry permits, deeds of adoption, and other legal documents—that

I could piece together the narrative of my Hawaiian lineage and, most important, tie it together through the story of the lāhui Hawaiʻi (the Hawaiian nation and people). It was especially via the moʻolelo of the lāhui Hawaiʻi as I learned it from the work of Lilikalā Kameʻeleihiwa, John Kamakawiwoʻole Osorio, and Noenoe Silva that the moʻolelo of my family became coherent (Kameʻeleihiwa 1992; Silva 2004; Osorio 2002). Disconnected individuals and episodes became part of the Kanaka Maoli past: the displacement of my Hawaiian ancestors by the Māhele, the intermarriage of my kūpunahine ʻŌiwi (indigenous female ancestors) with my Chinese male ancestors in the context of commercial expansion and Chinese settler colonialism in Hawaiʻi after the 1870s, and the multiple diasporic experiences of my Kanaka Maoli ancestors to China and North America (Fujikane and Okamura 2008).[1] The family narrative became meaningful to me through the narrative of the Native Hawaiian past.

Piecing together a comprehensible narrative is a crucial element of the methodology of moʻokūʻauhau. It is important to remember that two Hawaiian words are often treated as equivalents of the English word "genealogy": kūʻauhau and moʻokūʻauhau. Although they are often treated as synonyms, they are more usefully thought of as *near* synonyms. The first definition that the great scholars and lexicographers Mary Kawena Pukui and Samuel H. Elbert give for kūʻauhau is "genealogy," whereas moʻokūʻauhau they define first as "genealogical succession" (1986, 171, 254). Connotatively kūʻauhau suggests to me the ancestry itself, and moʻokūʻauhau suggests the narration of the ancestry. The difference between the two words is, of course, the moʻo. (See Lisa Kahaleole Hall's essay in this collection for her discussion of various Kanaka reflections on this term.) "He moʻo" means (among other important things) a succession or a series—something with a sequence. The placing of elements into a sequence creates a narrative meaning. The power of the moʻo becomes clearer when we think of another pair of words, ʻōlelo (language or word) and moʻolelo (story or history). It is moʻo that takes ʻōlelo (language) and turns it into moʻolelo, a narrative with meaning (Pukui and Elbert 1986, 253, 254). As Noelani Arista crucially notes, it does not place static limits on that meaning: "The very word *moʻo* or succession suggests that traditions and histories enlarge and adapt, and it also illustrates a built-in multiplicity native to Hawaiian oral tradition" (2007, xii). It is moʻo that takes kūʻauhau (ancestry) and turns it into moʻokūʻauhau (a tracing of a lineage in a series, a genealogical narrative) (Kauanui 2008, 37). The moʻo simultaneously makes meaning and opens up possibilities for multiple meanings.

But moʻo does not simply mean series; its meaning is much larger and its power is far greater. A moʻo is an ʻaumakua (an ancestral spirit), a water spirit, a female spirit, a lizard, a lizard god, and (again, according to Pukui and Elbert), an "enchanter." (1986, 253). Moʻo are the focus of ongoing research by Marie Alohalani Brown. This enchanter, the moʻo, has the power to reveal relationships between elements, relationships that might not otherwise be evident to the observer—especially if those relationships are denied by powerful, officially endorsed ideologies, as I will argue they are. In the case of understanding my own family through mo'okū'auhau, the mo'o brought meaning to the kū'auhau. By transcending the imposed fictions of the atomized individual and the bounded nation-state, mo'okū'auhau revealed that Native Hawaiian kūpuna who lived in Maunaoni in South Kona, who lived in Ooshek in South China, and my own Hawai'i-born father who lived in Milwaukee, were united as part of a larger Kanaka Maoli mo'olelo with a meaning.

In Indigenous studies, the individual is often an ideological and political construct to problematize and historicize. Scholars have traced the imposition of Western ideas of the individual in Native societies, a notion placed into practice through the individuation of land ownership (such as American Indian allotment or the Māhele division of Hawaiian lands as discussed by Lilikalā Kame'eleihiwa). They have explored the cultivation of individual subjectivity through Western education (such as the Kamehameha Schools' promotion of students' "individual 'self-government'" in the face of infringements on "the sovereignty of the Hawaiian nation," as discussed by Noelani Goodyear-Ka'ōpua). They have argued that the generation of individual blood quantum numbers has worked to fractionate Native nations (such as blood rolls in American Indian nations or quantum requirements of the Hawaiian Homelands Commission, as discussed by J. Kēhaulani Kauanui) (Pfister 2004; Doerfler 2009; Chang 2010, 78; Kame'eleihiwa 1992; Beaulieu 1984; Adams 1995; Goodyear-Ka'ōpua 2014, 36; Kauanui 2008, 37). It is not that Indigenous Studies or Hawaiian Studies deny the existence or dignity of human individuals. But a central strength of Indigenous Studies (including Hawaiian Studies, but also Indigenous Studies more broadly) can be and should be to problematize the now-dominant Western notion of the individual.

The classical Western liberalism of Adam Smith, John Locke, Thomas Jefferson, and others has shaped a concept of the individual that is part of a schema that disguises two repressive structures as vehicles of emancipation. Those two structures are, first, the allegedly "free" market (which claims to liberate individual economic actors, but has functioned to build the structure of capitalist exploitation of people and the environment) and, second, the supposedly egalitarian republic (which claims to be the creation of free individual citizens, but has functioned to institute imperial, settler colonial, and hetero-patriarchal modes of domination). Because mo'okū'auhau reveals the diasporic kinship networks that connect individuals across territorial boundaries, it has the power to give the lie to notions of the atomized individual and the coherent and bounded settler nation-state. In my case, this meant seeing past the isolating and atomizing ways that states presented my kūpuna. What appeared to be disconnected individuals (a Kanaka Maoli individual in Hawaiʻi, a Chinese individual in China) were actually part of a lineage whose very moʻolelo revealed that nation-states' allegedly stable territorial and racial boundaries are fictions. By using genealogical methods in historical research, I uncovered the transoceanic connections of Kanaka Maoli, Concow American Indian, and Chinese people (Chang 2011). Tracing connections lays bare the process of settler colonial and imperial boundary making, helping to denaturalize those boundaries.

Pulling our focus back from isolated individuals also opens up a deeper temporal perspective—a sense of the individual in time. Moʻokūʻauhau places the individual in a long-term narrative of succession, and within a network of kinship. Attending to descent and genealogy can permit a deeper historical understanding of both the imposing and eluding of racial, national, and colonial boundaries, and the sustaining of alternative geographies of connection. By tracing genealogy, we can see when and how boundaries were imposed: my ancestors were variously termed Hawaiians and Chinese by Hawaiian, American, and Chinese states and empires. Tracing genealogy also reveals how kūpuna eluded or subverted boundaries, as families retained connections to both Hawaiian and Chinese places, and both peoples and individuals frustrated governments' efforts to categorize them. Thus moʻokūʻauhau reveals the broad spatial context and deep chronological context in which people can be understood more fully and more truly. It can be a decolonial practice.

Here I distinguish between the potentially decolonial uses of indigenous moʻokūʻauhau and the potentially dangerous and reactionary practice of what we can call settler genealogy. Genealogical narratives (and the romantic images of families in the past that often accompany them) can easily fall into the sort of romantic nostalgia that hampers critical historical inquiry (Lowenthal 1985; Coontz 1992; Boym, 2001). Genealogical practices by white Americans since the 1960s, and the broader phenomenon of white ethnic revival out of which they emerged, can be fruitfully studied in the context of settler colonial studies. These genealogical practices have supported the identity claims of non-Native white people in the United States in three ways. First, non-Natives have used their families' genealogies to stake a claim to a sort of indigeneity, pointing toward the persistence of their lineages on the soil of North America. Second, this kind of genealogical research simultaneously allowed white Americans to use their own ethnicity (and often the ethnic discrimination their ancestors faced) to disavow responsibility for racism in the American past and present. Finally, genealogy and the white ethnic revival have permitted white Americans entry into privileged forms of romantic diasporic nationalism. Far from challenging the power of American nationalism, romantic diasporic nationalisms and settler genealogy ultimately reinforce it.

The process of using genealogy to reinforce settler power, and particularly the power of particular settler families, goes back far before the current American craze for genealogy. As María Elena Martínez, Francesca Morgan, and François Weil demonstrate, the practice stretches deep into the nineteenth century, and even precedes the establishment of independent settler nation-states (during the so-called "colonial periods" of U.S. and Mexican history) (Martínez 2008; Morgan 2010a, 2010b; Weil 2007).

The regulation of sexuality, and especially female reproductive sexuality, was at the heart of these settler genealogical processes, appearing in its attention to sexual reproduction and especially to the proving of "legitimacy"—reproduction exclusively within marital bonds (Rubin 1997; Engels 1902, 75–90). The study of the political uses of settler colonial genealogical discourses and practices demonstrates that they were foundational to settler colonialism in the past, support it in the present, and reflect the centrality of the regulation of sexuality to settler colonial societies.

Clearly, then, a decolonial process of moʻokūʻauhau must not emulate settler nationalist genealogy and its obsessions over legitimacy and sexual control. Just as clearly, moʻokūʻauhau draws on an independent Kanaka heritage that is full of liberatory possibility. As the work of Lilikalā Kameʻeihiwa and Noenoe Silva underscore, genealogy was the mode of history par excellence in classical Hawaiian society. The first historical works written in the Hawaiian language were genealogies: as Malcolm Nāea Chun has noted, the first published work by the great scholar Davida Malo were genealogies, and he, A. Unauna, Kaʻoʻo ʻAuwae, and Kamokuiki had begun recording genealogies in writing as early as 1827 (Chun 1993, 2). Granted, moʻokūʻauhau was an important tool for establishing and defending claims to power, both in ka wā ʻŌiwi wale (exclusively indigenous times prior to 1778) and then later as powerful Kānaka built and sought authority in a Hawaiian Kingdom and a Hawaiian state. But in the face of Westerners' colonialist ambitions in nineteenth-century Hawaiʻi, the practice of moʻokūʻauhau was of the essence in the defense of Kanaka Maoli sovereignty. It affirmed that the real basis of political legitimacy descended from Hawaiian, and not foreign, sources. As J. Kēhaulani Kauanui has demonstrated, in the face of U.S. federal debates in the 1920s over who would count as a Hawaiian in the distribution of homestead lands, Native Hawaiians continued to assert that the question of who counts as Native Hawaiian should depend on Indigenous genealogical practices. These practices, as Kauanui emphasizes, ignore Western notions of blood quantum in favor of Native practices of lineal descent (2008). It is in this crucial difference between moʻokūʻauhau's tracing of lineal descent and settler genealogy's policing of blood quantum that we can see why moʻokūʻauhau is a potentially liberatory practice. As Lisa Kahaleole Hall has argued, moʻokūʻauhau separates Native Hawaiians from the usurpations of non-Hawaiian "Hawaiians at heart" (2005). Up to the present day, Kānaka continue to practice forms of genealogy that place moʻokūʻauhau at the center of Hawaiian history, identity, and politics (Kauanui 2007; Schachter 2008; Iaukea 2011; Chang 2011).

It is essential to note that moʻokūʻauhau (like all historical narration) is a creative act of selection: it is the active *making* of a selective narrative of descent, not merely the discovery of a truth that lies buried in the archives. As Jocelyn Linnekin puts it, "Hawaiian genealogical reckoning, with its myriad possibilities and entwining paths, in itself carries considerable potential for play" (1990). But as Linnekin knows well, this is serious play, and selection is its operative mechanism. Moʻokūʻauhau is not merely unearthing the true names of ancestors, but selecting the ancestral lines we will trace in order to get at some generative truth. In Kingdom times and before, moʻokūʻauhau was in large part a political art and a chiefly practice. Along with valor in war and sexual relations with a chief of high status, moʻokūʻauhau was a means to increased mana (spiritual power) that was important to rank in the society. Moʻokūʻauhau was often used to establish the truth that one was descended from an illustrious ancestor of great mana and high rank, had inherited some of this mana, and were entitled to some of the rank that went with it (Kameʻeleihiwa 1992, 44–47; Silva 2004, 93).

Today, rank is no longer a prime motivator for researching moʻokūʻauhau, and moʻokūʻauhau instead affirms one's ancestral belonging to particular families, particular places, and most of all to the indigenous lāhui Hawaiʻi more broadly. Thus moʻokūʻauhau today tends to emphasize the Kanaka Maoli lines from which Kānaka descend, rather than the settlers among their ancestors (although there is fruitful work to be done in using moʻokūʻauhau to interrogate the relations between Maoli and settlers). This act of creation by tracing selected Kanaka Maoli lines asserts indigenous continuity between the Native Hawaiian past and the Native Hawaiian present.

This affirmation powerfully rejects the colonialist notion that Kānaka today are not "authentic" and thus have no special claim to their homeland, the Hawaiian Islands. Outsiders have claimed that because Kānaka today may not speak Hawaiian, may not live in ways that outsiders imagine and define as "traditional," or may not have some level of "blood quantum," they are not truly indigenous. This is a slander on the individual, but it is also an attack on Kānaka Maoli more generally. By outsiders' measures of authenticity such as these, there are few, or perhaps no, true Native Hawaiian people today. Why then, outsiders ask, should Kānaka Maoli wield any power in their own homeland? It is no exaggeration to call these reductionist metrics of authenticity not only colonialist, but also genocidal. The practice of moʻokūʻauhau and the process of selectivity that it entails offer a powerful response by asserting the continuity of contemporary Kānaka with their kūpuna and the rejection of reductionist metrics of blood and authenticity (Kauanui 2008, 194–196). Even though moʻokūʻauhau is practiced to trace the lineages of particular people, it is a broader political practice that demonstrates the continuity of the Kanaka Maoli past, present, and future. The tracing of reproductive ancestry and the demonstration of ancestral belonging to the broader community of Kānaka Maoli are thus important and decolonial political acts.

Yet moʻokūʻauhau can be an even more powerfully liberatory practice when we recall that Kānaka and other Pacific Islanders have long embraced expansive ideas and practices of lineage and kinship. These ideas and practices extend far beyond the questions of biological reproduction and reproductive legitimacy that lie at the historical roots of settler genealogical practices. Recent scholarship by Hokulani Aikau, Kealani Cook, and (from Māori studies) Alice Te Punga Somerville follows a course charted by the resurgence of Pacific voyaging traditions since the 1970s when they demonstrate the dense web of ties that knit Pacific Islanders together (Aikau 2012; Cook 2011; Somerville 2012). Ty P. Kāwika Tengan, Tēvita O. Kaʻili, and Rochelle Tuitagavaʻa Fonoti have worked together "to create a new genealogy for Indigenous anthropology in/of Oceania" (Tengan, Kaʻili, and Fonoti 2010). In my own work, I trace the ways that nineteenth-century Kānaka drew upon stories, language, sacred tradition, and spirituality in acts of comparative auto-ethnography to delineate that a common origin bound them to kindred peoples in the Pacific (Chang 2016). We can see that many of today's scholars and their intellectual kūpuna as performing acts of moʻokūʻauhau that reaffirm that Hawaiʻi is part of what Epeli Hauʻofa has termed "a sea of islands" united by the Pacific Ocean—not separate specks of land (2008). This is moʻokūʻauhau writ large at the spatial level.

If moʻokūʻauhau can be as expansive at the conceptual level, especially as we think of lineage and kinship, its interpretive and political power grows even greater. The Hawaiian notion of lineage has been, is, and must continue to be broader than settler genealogy's restrictive and heteronormative notion of reproductive descent. Moʻokūʻauhau is a means to reclaim and shed light on social ties that are denied by individuating colonial policies, discouraged by liberal and neoliberal legal structures, and interrupted by the boundaries that empires and settler states have drawn around Kānaka and others. Note that the demonstration of the power of these ties of kinship and these narratives of genealogy often succeed best when they point to the many enduring bonds between Kānaka that states deny are real. Hānai adoption, calling one another auntie and uncle and cousin and braddah and sistah—all of this is what anthropologists call "fictive kinship." The same term might apply to the bonds between ʻaikane (same-sex intimate comrades) and the connections deepened by the practice of hoʻokāne (the adoption by a woman of "a man as a platonic friend" that "cements friendship between the relatives of both participants") (Pukui and Elbert 1986, 128). By the same external measure, the enduring ties created between kumu hula (hula masters) and hula sisters and between kumu kula (schoolteachers) and their haumāna (students) are similarly fictive as well.

But we must resist the notion that such bonds are "fictive," because no kinship exists outside the narratives that construct it—even if we call that narrative "blood." The term "fictive kinship" immediately invokes "the real," underscoring that critical feminist and gender studies of the family are essential to the study of kinship and genealogy (Cott 2000; Pascoe 2009). As Kath Weston has argued, state-endorsed normative kinship practices of heterosexual marriage and reproduction have the romance of "the real" (1995). That romance has sometimes shaped the way that sexually dissident people have figured their kinship, creating a norm to which to aspire—for example, the forms of heterosexual marriage. (Note, however that Lisa Duggan, the scholar most associated with the term homonormativity, writes that "there is no structure for gay life, no matter how conservative or normalizing, that might compare with the institutions promoting and sustaining heterosexual coupling" [2003, 94, n. 15].) In addition to fragmenting queer communities, this romance of "real" (heterosexual) kinship has obscured the reality that non-heterosexual people have elaborated their own kinship practices in various historical contexts. Understanding genealogy on these different terms could profoundly enrich our understanding of the history of sexually dissident communities.

Similarly, contemporary Kānaka can imagine moʻokūʻauhau in this expansive way—all in addition to a tracing of fathers, mothers, and biological offspring. There is great power in refusing to limit our moʻokūʻauhau to Christian heteronormative family lines. The classical practice of moʻokūʻauhau traced lines of sexual reproduction, but these were part of a large and complex network of lines of descent and connection of all sorts— intellectual, political, sexual, ʻoihana (skilled craft or profession), and more. Kānaka today are imagining moʻōkūʻauhau as a practice that helps us to see and to rebuild connections that link Kānaka together in ways that cross colonially imposed boundaries of the individual and of the settler nation-state and reveal how Kānaka have and still do continue their lineage in ways that go far beyond the state-sanctioned bonds of heterosexual reproduction.

My own family's history was illegible to me because colonially imposed boundaries of nationality, authenticity, and race obscured the connection between individuals. Learning the moʻolelo of the Hawaiian nation and researching moʻokūʻauhau was a transgressive practice that demonstrated the narrative of family that spanned boundaries, revealed kinship networks, and placed individuals in time. Whereas settler colonial practices of genealogy affirm settler identity claims and reinforce the legitimacy of settler states, my experience demonstrated to me that moʻokūʻauhau can be a decolonial methodology, especially when we hearken to the richness of Kanaka lineage and kinship practices. We make our moʻokūʻauhau by selection. If we embrace

Kanaka notions of expansive kinship and lineage rather than confine ourselves to imported notions of legitimacy and heterosexual reproduction, we can make an expansive and transgressive and liberatory moʻokūʻauhau. We can trace the connections that states and empires cannot determine and cannot always even perceive. We can embrace ancestors and kin who we might not otherwise know. Moʻokūʻauhau in all its fullness can be a powerfully liberating practice of transgression that spreads widely through space and reaches deeply into time, connecting us to kūpuna long dead and moʻopuna not yet born.

Notes

I would like to thank Nālani Wilson-Hokowhitu, Lisa Kahaleole Hall, Marie Alohalani Brown, and my colleagues Tracey Deutsch, Kevin Murphy, and Ann Waltner for their invaluable suggestions for this essay.

1. The literature on Asian settler colonialism in Hawaiʻi emphasizes the role of Japanese settlers, but the concept is also useful in analyzing the place of Chinese settlers.

References

Adams, David Wallace. 1995. *Education for Extinction: American Indians and the Boarding School Experience, 1875–1928*. Lawrence: University Press of Kansas.

Aikau, Hokulani K. 2012. *Chosen People, Promised Land: Mormonism and Race in Hawaiʻi*. Minneapolis: University of Minnesota Press.

Arista, Noelani. 2007. "Foreword." In *Kepelino's Traditions of Hawaiʻi*, edited by Mary Warren Beckwith, pp. i–xiv. Honolulu: Bishop Museum Press.

Beaulieu, David L. 1984. "Curly Hair and Big Feet: Physical Anthropology and the Implementation of Land Allotment on the White Earth Chippewa Reservation." *American Indian Quarterly* 8, no. 4 (Autumn): 281–314.

Boym, Svetlana. 2001. *The Future of Nostalgia*. New York: Basic Books.

Chang, David A. 2011. "Borderlands in a World at Sea: Concow Indians, Native Hawaiians, and South Chinese in Indigenous, Global, and National Space, 1860s–1880s." *Journal of American History* 98, no. 2 (September): 384–403.

———. 2010. *The Color of the Land: Race, Nation, and the Politics of Landownership in Oklahoma, 1832–1929*. Chapel Hill: University of North Carolina Press.

Chun, Malcolm Nāea. 1993. *Nā Kukui Pio ʻOle: The Inextinguishable Torches*. Honolulu: First People's Productions.

Cook, Kealani. 2011. "Kahiki: Native Hawaiian Relationships with Other Pacific Islanders." PhD diss., University of Michigan, Ann Arbor.

Coontz, Stephanie. 1992. *The Way We Never Were: American Families and the Nostalgia Trap*. New York: BasicBooks.

Cott, Nancy. 2000. *Public Vows: A History of Marriage and the Nation*. Cambridge, MA: Harvard University Press.

Doerfler, Jill. 2009. "An Anishinaabe Tribalography: Investigating and Interweaving Conceptions of Identity during the 1910s on the White Earth Reservation." *American Indian Quarterly* 33, no. 3 (Summer): 295–324

Duggan, Lisa. 2003. *The Twilight of Equality: Neoliberalism, Cultural Politics, and the Attack on Democracy.* Boston: Beacon, 2003.

Engels, Friedrich. 1902. *The Origins of the Family: Private Property and the State.* Chicago: Charles H. Kerr.

Fujikane, Candace, and Jonathan Y. Okamura, eds. 2008. *Asian Settler Colonialism: From Local Governance to the Habits of Everyday Life in Hawaiʻi.* Honolulu: University of Hawaiʻi Press.

Goodyear-Kaʻōpua, Noelani. 2014. "Domesticating Hawaiians: Kamehameha Schools and the 'Tender Violence' of Marriage." In *Indian Subjects: Hemispheric Perspectives on the History of Indigenous Education,* edited by Brenda Child and Brian Klapotek, pp. 16–47. Santa Fe: School for Advanced Research.

Hall, Lisa Kahaleole. 2005. "'Hawaiian at Heart' and Other Fictions." *The Contemporary Pacific* 17, no. 2:404–413.

Hauʻofa, Epeli. 2008. "Our Sea of Islands." In *We Are the Ocean: Collected Works.* Honolulu: University of Hawaiʻi Press, pp. 27–40.

Iaukea, Sidney L. 2011. *The Queen and I: A Story of Dispossessions and Reconnections in Hawaiʻi.* Berkeley: University of California Press.

Kameʻeleihiwa, Lilikalā. 1992. *Native Land and Foreign Desire: Pehea Lā e Pono Ai?* Honolulu: University of Hawaiʻi Press.

Kauanui, J. Kēhaulani. 2007. "Diasporic Deracination and 'Off-Island' Hawaiians." *The Contemporary Pacific* 19, no. 1:138–160.

———. 2008. *Hawaiian Blood: Colonialism and the Politics of Sovereignty and Indigeneity.* Durham, NC: Duke University Press.

Linnekin, Jocelyn. 1990. *Sacred Queens and Women of Consequence: Rank, Gender, and Colonialism in the Hawaiian Islands.* Ann Arbor: University of Michigan Press.

Lowenthal, David. 1985. *The Past Is a Foreign Country.* Cambridge: Cambridge University Press.

Martínez, María Elena. 2008. *Genealogical Fictions: Limpieza de Sangre, Religion, and Gender in Colonial Mexico.* Stanford, CA: Stanford University Press.

Morgan, Francesca. 2010a. "Lineage as Capital: Genealogy in Antebellum New England." *New England Quarterly.* 83, no. 2 (June): 250–282.

———. 2010b. "A Noble Pursuit? The Embourgeoisement of Genealogy, and Genealogy's Making of the Bourgeoisie." In *The American Bourgeoisie: Distinction and Identity in the Nineteenth Century,* edited by Sven Beckert and Julia B. Rosenbaum, pp. 135–151. New York: Palgrave Macmillan.

Osorio, Jon Kamakawiwoʻole. 2002. *Dismembering Lāhui: A History of the Hawaiian Nation to 1887.* Honolulu: University of Hawaiʻi Press.

Pascoe, Peggy. 2009. *What Comes Naturally: Miscegenation Law and the Making of Race in America.* Oxford: Oxford University Press.

Pfister, Joel. 2004. *Individuality Incorporated: Indians and the Multicultural Modern.* Durham, NC: Duke University Press.

Pukui, Mary Kawena, and Samuel H. Elbert. 1986. *Hawaiian Dictionary.* Honolulu: University of Hawaiʻi Press, 1986.

Rubin, Gayle. 1997. "The Traffic in Women: Notes on the 'Political Economy' of Sex."
In *The Second Wave: A Reader in Feminist Theory*, edited by Linda Nicholson, pp.
27–62. New York: Routledge.

Schachter, Judith. 2008. "A Relationship Endeared to the People: Adoption in Hawaiian
Custom and Law." *Pacific Studies* 31, no. 3/4 (September/December): 211–231.

Silva, Noenoe K. 2004. *Aloha Betrayed: Native Hawaiian Resistance to American
Colonialism*. Durham, NC: Duke University Press.

Somerville, Alice Te Punga. 2012. *Once Were Pacific: Māori Connections to Oceania*.
Minneapolis: University of Minnesota Press.

Tengan, Ty P. Kāwika, Tēvita O. Kaʻili, and Rochelle Tuitagavaʻa Fonoti. 2010.
"Genealogies: Articulating Indigenous Anthropology in/of Oceania." *Pacific
Studies* 33, no. 2/3 (August/December): 139–167.

Weil, François. 2007. "John Farmer and the Making of American Genealogy." *New
England Quarterly* 80, no. 3 (September): 408–434.

Weston, Kath. 1995. "Forever Is a Long Time: Romancing the Real in Gay Kinship
Ideologies." In *Naturalizing Power: Essays in Feminist Cultural Analysis*, edited by
Sylvia Yanagisako and Carole Delaney, pp. 87–112. New York: Routledge.

8

ALL OUR RELATIONS

Moʻokūʻauhau and Moʻolelo

LISA KAHALEOLE HALL

This collection expands on the possibilities of using moʻokūʻauhau as methodology, in the hopes that exploring the very different places we come from, both literally and figuratively, will map directions for our future work and relationships in the world. My contribution to our collective conversation is to reflect on the relationship between moʻokūʻauhau (genealogy), moʻolelo (story), and kuleana (responsibility/authority to act). I come to this conversation as a multiracial Kanaka Maoli woman who grew up in the U.S. military and has spent life thus far traveling from place to place trying to make connections with all kinds of others. My Hawaiian connections and those beyond Hawaiʻi are deep and wide, and await understanding their layered meanings; moʻokūʻauhau for me means missionaries and kāhuna, educators and voyagers, the remembered and the unspoken, the living and the dead.

The Hawaiian meaning of the name Kahaleole has been a double-edged sword for me, with its dual evocation of being without a house and thus homeless, and of having no single house and thus finding homes everywhere. Long ago, Kuʻumealoha Gomes was the first to tell me of a famous chanter Kahaleole who traveled from island to island telling stories. I have been reflecting on the meaning of this ever since. In the first part of my life, I felt the sense of homelessness and loss most acutely, moving from place to place without ever having another Hawaiian in my daily life besides my mother. In the second part of my life, I have focused more on appreciating the many peoples who have taken me in and the many homes where I have found a place. I am deeply grateful for Black kinship, women-of-color kinship, Pacific kinship, indigenous kinship, queer kinship, and many other forms of relationship that my diasporic life have allowed. I am finally positioning the richness of those connections at the center of my thinking and writing.

Many years ago, I wrote a poem about connections of loss and return for someone I understood to be another multiracial Kanaka woman; its final line was "Our diaspora has not been gifted with a name." Twenty years later, our diaspora has been gifted with so very many names, as diasporic Hawaiians return to the islands, and as the island-born and island-raised are forced or choose to move outward to gain access to housing, education, and employment. Many more commit themselves to relearning 'Ōlelo Hawai'i and thus gain access to the rich heritage of oral and written history our Kanaka ancestors left for us, knowing we would need it. As I write, I am surrounded by voices coming through today's technologies of Facebook postings, community-access television, and Internet live streaming of meetings held by the U.S. Department of the Interior. They are asking the Hawaiian community whether federal recognition of a "nation to nation" relationship between the United States and a "Hawaiian governing body" should be created, within the framework of that terrible and ludicrous fiction of "domestic dependent" nationhood invented by the U.S. Supreme Court and imposed on the native nations of the continental United States. Almost all the speakers from every island that came to the forums reached backward and forward in time, recognizing the echo in these 2014 hearings of the historical record that Noenoe Silva brought back to us from the backrooms of the U.S. National Archives ('Ōlelo TV 2014). Silva's (2004a) recovery of the Kū'ē petitions of 1897 document that the majority of surviving Hawaiians registered their strong objections to the illegal annexation of our nation and their desire for the injustice to be rectified. Her historical work supported a very different story than what white American historians, like Gavan Daws, taught, asserting Hawaiian acquiescence and/or indifference to the overthrow of the Kingdom of Hawai'i. This more accurate story has heartened and sustained the sovereignty activism of today with its documentation of our genealogy of struggle. It also raises different issues of kuleana. What is our responsibility to this knowledge?

In Hawaiian metaphorical terms, we face forward toward the past. Ka wā mamua lies before us; it does not lie behind. Neither the past nor the future is linear; we gain knowledge of our roots to shape our present and our futures. William Faulkner's famous assertion, "The past is never dead. It's not even past," reflects an aspect of this knowledge. Moʻokūʻauhau and moʻolelo are fundamentally intertwined

Hawaiians in Unexpected Places

Our voyaging ancestors are everywhere I look. I think about the Hawaiʻi delegations crossing the continent with the petitions of lāhui to plead their case against U.S. annexation in Washington, D.C. I see the footage from the train in Nā Maka o ka ʻĀina's re-creation of the queen's journey in the 1993 documentary "Act of War," with narration from her letters. The queen's voice still lives in Hawaiian memory through both her writings and songs. She valued education as did all the other Kānaka, aliʻi and makaʻāinana alike, who flocked to the missionary schools in search of literacy, perhaps even more than for the words of Jesus. By the mid-1800s, only thirty years after the missionaries first brought the written word to the islands, the Kanaka Maoli literacy rate was among the highest in the world, a statistic that no longer holds, due to the depredations of colonial education systems. In Noenoe Silva's important essay on the politics of Hawaiian language and history "I Kū Mau Mau: How Kānaka Maoli Tried To Sustain National Identity Within the United States Political System," she cites Larry Kimura's fact-finding in the 1983 Native Hawaiians Study Commission:

> As part of making Hawaiʻi into an outpost of the United States,
> the Hawaiian language was attacked most vigorously, and "at
> its most vulnerable and important point," in the school system.
> "Hawaiian was strictly forbidden anywhere within school yards
> or buildings and physical punishment for using it could be harsh.
> Teachers who were native speakers of Hawaiian were threatened
> with dismissal." Young Kanaka children were even punished for
> failing to understand English on the first day of school. (1983,
> 182–184)

Growing up, I had thought of my Hawaiian family as working class/lower middle class, but as I grew older I better understood our connections to educational power and community institutions within the history of the Hawaiian response to Western colonialism. I began to see that far from my being the educational anomaly I often felt while being isolated in my own colonial institutions of knowledge production, being an educator ran throughout my family history, past and present. My mother and her cousins grew up to teach K–12, and my great-grandmother was a housemother at the Kamehameha School for Girls. Alone in the archives of the Newberry Library in Chicago many years ago, I browsed through missionary journals and came upon the congratulations lauded on my great-great-great-grandfather, James

Kekela. He was an early convert and the first Kanaka Maoli missionary to the Marquesas, assigned by U.S. president Abraham Lincoln; J. Kēhaulani Kauanui wrote to tell me of seeing the mention of my great-grandmother Nora Kahaleole Chang in Smithsonian archives as a native informant on Hawaiian and Chinese admixture for the sociologists eager to theorize about Hawai'i's "melting pot"; I found a 1940s letter in a much copied set of family documents inquiring about an ancestor in the California Gold Rush who had begun calling himself "Jim Crow." I wonder which of my ancestors' lives are reflected in the iconic anthropological text, *The Polynesian Family System in Kā-'u* by Mary Kawena Pukui. Kā'u holds roots I have yet to explore, my grandmother raised away from her own mother, who was sent to the "leper colony" of Kalaupapa on the island of Moloka'i without my grandmother's knowledge.

The queen's historical support of the women's seminary that became Mills College in Oakland, California, meant that as I taught my first classes as an adjunct lecturer I crossed streets named in her honor. In northern California, and up through western Canada, Kānaka arrival and intermarriage with native North Americans is described in story and song. My friend and comrade, Kealoha Blake, and his nonprofit media center worked with filmmaker, Kat High, to document traditional stories of the Rainbow Bridge connecting the islands of Hawai'i to the Kahshia Pomo people on the West Coast of Turtle Island (Crossing Over Rainbow Bridge: Our Story 2001). Even in the gray flatness of midwestern Ohio, I came upon the story of Lydia Ka'ōnohiponiponiokalani Aholo, Lili'uokalani's only hanai daughter, sent to Oberlin to learn music and more, which she brought back home to share (Bonura and Witmer 2013). I see a photo of her dressed in Victorian garb on a wooden porch, present but not part of Oberlin's own black-and-white historical narrative. I went to Yale for my own undergraduate education but heard and knew nothing of Henry 'Ōpūkaha'ia and his fellow Kanaka students there in the midst of the missionaries and profiteers whose names were inscribed into the stone and brick buildings surrounding me (Demos 2014).

Our diasporas are not new; they are under-recorded, misread, or ignored. Our connections across time and place are about leaving and returning to Hawai'i nei, leaving and never returning, and forever staying. All deeply rooted in place.

A Genealogy of Sharing Knowledge

When I began my PhD work at the University of California at Berkeley, the ethnic studies graduate group had only existed for three years. Though the program was explicitly created to be cross-racial and multidisciplinary, all of its faculty were mono-disciplinarily trained and focused on a single racial grouping. Thus graduate students were often left to create our own paradigms and ways to connect the disparate narratives we were taught. The three existing cohorts contained a multitude of individuals, Native, Asian, Chicano, Caribbean, African American, and two white students, with very different histories and interests, who came from a wide range of racial, ethnic, geographical, and political histories. For the most part our differences were lateral, not hierarchical; there was no sense of overt competition. We supported each other within the classroom and without. We all knew that our previous educations had been impoverished by the racial segregation, censorship, and omissions of our previous curriculum. We all saw ourselves as part of the solution to that history in what we were learning and then teaching. The sense of solidarity and purpose that existed did not strike me as particularly notable at the time, partly because of the external assaults we were facing in the first round of the anti- "multiculturalism" wars of the late 1980s and early 1990s. We learned with and from each other, proximity enabling informal learning that is often more powerful than that of the classroom, or at least allowing the classroom learning to be more fully realized.

But as I have noted before, in this new interdisciplinary and multiracial PhD program that grew out of a history of community struggle there was no curriculum that addressed Hawai'i or U.S. colonial relations with other Pacific Islands as significant and foundational to understanding the development of the United States. One of the founding faculty of the ethnic studies graduate group, historian Ron Takaki, structured his Hawaiian language entitled study of labor in Hawai'i, *Pau Hana* (meaning the end of a workday), around the arrival of Asian immigrants within the plantation system (Takaki 1984). In this book, the only one in the core curriculum to discuss Hawai'i at all, Takaki relegates Native Hawaiian history and issues to a few, short paragraphs. During my undergraduate and graduate education, all the knowledge I gained and shared about indigenous Hawaiians and other Pacific Islanders came through personal and community relationships that led to extracurricular research, political organizing, and community outreach work. As I noted in my first public acknowledgment of this intellectual debt in my 2009 essay, "Navigating Our Own 'Sea of Islands,'" the 1990s organizing and cultural work of J. Kēhaulani Kauanui, Sharon Nawahine Lum Ho, Paul Kealoha Blake of the East Bay Media Center, Hinano Compton, Teresia Teaiwa, Patrick Makuakāne, kumu hula of Nā Lei Hulu I Ka Wēkiu, the Bay Area Pacific Islanders' Cultural Association, the Hayward Hula Festival, the 'Ohana Cultural Center, and La Peña Cultural Center in Oakland, California, were especially important to my political and intellectual development.

In the 1990s, before the death of affirmative action in the University of California, J. Kēhaulani Kauanui and I participated in a forum on bringing Pacific Island studies into the University of California system, hosted by a faculty member based in textile design. A large group of California community college students desperate for some knowledge of themselves and their communities attended. Surrounded by Tongan and Samoan young men, each well over six feet tall, I felt sure this was the largest concentration of Pacific Islander students that had ever convened in a University of California setting. They passionately wanted a teacher, but I had to tell them that I could not be that person because I had no real knowledge of them and their histories.

In contrast, I had been fortunate enough to be taken under the wing of the late Caribbean American feminist Barbara Christian, a deeply cherished mentor who later became my dissertation chair. Though she had no real knowledge of or deep interest in Pacific issues, she had a generous capacity for supporting a wide range of intellectual projects.

As a literary critic who both loved artists and appreciated the materiality of cultural production, and as a scholar fully cognizant of the urgent need to pass our knowledge on, Barbara had a profound impact on my intellectual development, as she did for so many other students across all racial-ethnic and disciplinary lines. The literature, fiction, creative nonfiction, poetry, and polemics of Black community, Black feminism, and African American studies helped decolonize my mind. My undergraduate work in women's studies at Yale had helped me articulate the commonplace socially unacknowledged misogyny and sexism surrounding me. Yet, Yale was weak on issues of race and class, except for the interventions of Matthews Hamabata, my undergraduate advisor and mentor, a "local" Japanese man who grew up on Kaua'i and whose mother and sister ran a restaurant there that my grandparents loved to visit. Without him, all of my undergraduate women's studies professors at Yale would have been white women. His courses were also a fundamentally important site in shaping my understanding of the world. It was in his classroom that I first heard the silence of reflection and communion, not erasure and exclusion.

Barbara showed her students that pleasure and beauty were legitimately desirable elements of art and scholarship; that art and politics were not separate arenas, and as she pointed out in her critically undervalued essay, "The Race for Theory," that "the finger pointing out the moon is not the moon" (Christian 1987, 52–53). That essay reminded us that peoples of color have always theorized, and that the many rich forms of that theorizing have been overshadowed at best, or delegitimized at worst, by the constant invocation of one very particular genealogy of theory originating in France and Germany and glossed as High Theory in the U.S. academy. If she had lived long enough to share this discussion, Barbara would have deeply appreciated the work on moʻokūʻauhau. She would have been an invaluable participant in the kinds of cross-community intellectual and political dialogues between Caribbeanists, African Americanists, Indigenous studies, and Pacific studies scholars that are only now beginning to blossom.

Moʻolelo

What stories do we tell? What stories do we know, and with whom do we decide to share them? The power of the word is a theme that cuts across all cultures, whether the concept of "nommo" held by the Dogon people of Mali or the ʻōlelo noʻeau recorded by Mary Kawena Pukui, "I ka ʻōlelo nō ke ola, i ka ʻōlelo nō ka make. In the word there is life, in the word there is death" (Pukui 1983, 129).

Canadian writer Thomas King's "truth about stories" in his collection of the same name is that "that's all we are." Each of the stories he proffers in his book is very different, but all end in the same way, the story is a gift that you can do with what you will, including forgetting it (King 2008).

Anishnaabe writer Leanne Simpson says,

> Storytelling is like air. It's that important, especially as a tool of decolonization and transformation. Stories have spirit and power and come to us as small gifts of wisdom, but they only have power if the ones that hear those stories, embody them and act. Stories are about responsibility and action in Indigenous cultures. They have kept us alive, grounded and inspired. They carry the resistance and the strength of our ancestors. They hold our truths. And when we tell them on our own terms to an engaged audience, they carry a tremendous responsibility to Transform. (2014)

Kuʻualoha Hoʻomanawanui, Brandy Nālani McDougall, and Marie Alohalani Brown are the most recent wahine Kanaka ʻŌiwi to take on the work of connecting English language scholarship and moʻolelo, building on the work of Noenoe Silva and Lilikalā Kameʻeleihiwa. Hoʻomanawanui's *Voices of Fire: Reweaving the Literary Lei of Pele and Hiʻiaka* reclaims the stories of these titular goddesses that colonial renditions trivialized and distorted. She brings them back into a Hawaiian political and cultural context of resistance and continuity, a "literary *moʻokūʻauhau*" as its publisher describes it. McDougall's poetry re-narrates the cosmological kinship of humans, places, and spirits. Michelle Peek writes of McDougall's poem "Hāloanaka" from her collection *The Salt-Wind/Ka Makani Paʻakai*: "the water that passes through the taro plant infuses all manner of kinship, economic, and social relations in Hawaiʻi, connecting Kānaka Maoli to their ancestor Hāloa, and to land, sea, and each other, as well as through the formative oceanic movements of Moana Nui to other Pacific Islanders" (Peek 2013, 80). Brown's MA thesis explores how the predominantly female moʻo deities of Hawaiʻi embody the hoʻola (life-giving) and hoʻomake (death-dealing properties) of the water element with which they are associated. She notes that "like water, they slip through your fingers when you try to grasp them. Replicating the elusive nature of moʻo, fragments of knowledge about these reptilian water deities lurk here and there, sometimes in unexpected places, but more often, they are hidden deep within our epic moʻolelo, many of which are not easily accessible today for one reason or another" (Kohala Center 2012).

Brown's emphasis on the moʻo portion of moʻolelo was prefigured by the work of Mary Kawena Pukui and Adrienne Kaeppler that J. Kēhaulani Kauanui reflects upon in her book *Hawaiian Blood*:

> Moʻo is also the word for lizard and lizard-like supernatural beings. The imagery of the *moʻo* lizard with visible vertebrae and *kua moʻo* (vertebrae backbone, or to link something together) "is apt and obvious as a simile for sequence of descendants in contiguous unbroken articulation," where one traces his or her genealogy in steps, just as one can follow the vertebrae of the spine (Handy and Pukui 1972, 197; Kaeppler 1982, 85). It is interesting to note that the word ʻauhau is used to mean an assessment, tribute, levy, or tax, which indicates the reciprocal relationship between the common people, the chiefs, and the land. (2008, 37)

Moʻokūʻauhau is an active story. There is always a choice of who will be acknowledged in what contexts and which webs of relation will be prioritized. The activity is crucial in creating and reinforcing both relationships and knowledge. The knowledge of the storyteller is both communal and unique to the person, one-voiced and multidimensional, and uttered in the present while invoking past and future. Stories help us remember who we are and how we are related but they also create those relationships.

A Story of "Our Sea of Islands"

In other work, I have gone into detail about the negative consequences for Pacific Islanders of the U.S. continental use of the terms "Asian Pacific," "Asian Pacific Islander," and "API" by Asian Americans and other non-Pacific people (Hall 2015). The most fundamental consequence is that Pacific Islander stories are either absent or deeply distorted within this framing. In response to this, Tongan and Samoan community activists and social service providers worked with the Peninsula Violence Prevention Center in San Mateo, California, to convene the First Annual Pacific Islander Anti-Violence conference in June 2014. The conference was historic for a number of painful reasons. It was the first time Samoans, Tongans, Hawaiians, Fijians, and Chamorro met together as a group named "Pacific Islander" to tell their stories of community violence. The specifics of Samoan, Tongan, Hawaiian, Fijian, and Chamorro issues with police and gang violence, domestic and sexual violence, and homophobic and gender violence were at the center of the conference, not absent nor an add-on at the periphery of an "API" framing where Asian American issues and statistics form the majority, if not totality, of analysis and discussion. At the most basic level, simply to be in a room filled with Pacific Islander bodies from more than one community was an experience most of the attendees had never been able to have in a U.S. context. I use the term "bodies" here because differential embodiment is a significant part of the group experience within the United States. Though of course there are differences of size, skin color, hair texture, and height within self-defined Asian American and Pacific Islander groups, if you juxtapose them, the physical differences between the two groups are a marker of the social and political differences of their embodiment in a white supremacist racial system, "perpetual alien" vs. noble or threatening savage, for example.

I began my conference keynote by noting that Pacific Islanders are not Asian Americans, and highlighting the fact that when Asian Americans and other non–Pacific Islander groups use the terminology of "API" they are almost always using Hawaiians to stand in for the Pacific. I called on my fellow Kānaka Maoli, in hopes that the existence and particularities of other Islanders are not erased in this practice, and for all of us from various Pacific nations to reflect on our ignorance of each other's lives produced by our colonial educations. In then asking who Pacific Islanders are, I paid homage to the foundational work of Epeli Hau'ofa, Tongan artist, intellectual, and cultural critic, who demonstrated our diverse connections in both his work and life. Born in Papua New Guinea, schooled there and in Tonga and Fiji, Hau'ofa died as a citizen of Fiji. His cultural work explored how we are related across the Pacific through voyaging and connecting through land and sea, but this relation is not to say we are identical. This distinction is key to how I think about mo'okū'auhau as methodology. It is about relatedness and difference. Hau'ofa's life work also reveals the centrality of mo'olelo, storytelling, to understanding who we are and how we have been, are now, and could be related to others. In combination or alone, mo'okū'auhau and mo'olelo are neither static nor univocal. After my keynote, an attendee excitedly told me she was related to Hau'ofa and had been texting his sister in Papua New Guinea while I was speaking that he was being honored at the conference. I took and uploaded a picture of myself and my new sister from Fiji onto Facebook upon hearing this and Teresia Teaiwa immediately responded with a query about her, posting from her home in Aotearoa (New Zealand) across oceans and time zones. Teaiwa, born of African American and Pacific Islander (Banaban, I-Kiribati) parents and raised in Fiji, was hired by Hau'ofa to teach at the University of the South Pacific for her first full-time academic appointment. After obtaining her PhD from the University of California at Santa Cruz program that also graduated Vince Diaz and J. Kēhaulani Kauanui, she went on to help develop one of the strongest Pacific Studies programs in the world as a Senior Lecturer in Pacific Studies at Victoria University. Her untimely death in 2017 was mourned around the world as reminders of her irreplaceable capabilities for relationship building and solidarity mounted. Poets, teachers, students, and activists hold up her memory and ongoing influence as the Pacific loops circle, intertwine, in time and space.

Teresia's influence on her multidimensional web of relations demonstrates the profound importance of genealogy, both formal and informal, to Hawaiians and other Pacific Islanders. When two Hawaiians come together who have not met before, the question of how they are related is front and center, whether through family, geography, schooling, or friendship networks. This is an important reason for the success of Mormon missionaries throughout the Pacific. The Mormon theological belief that one can pray one's ancestors into heaven retroactively requires a deep interest in genealogy and knowledge of who those ancestors are to accomplish this. Mormon temples all have extensive genealogical archives that both Mormon faithful and non-Mormons can and do consult. Ceremonially, the recitation of one's own personal genealogy before speaking publicly is a method of grounding the discussion in relationship and place, and potentially offers others a means of connection to the speaker and/or a deeper context for the speaking that follows. It can also be an assertion of pride and cultural authority through both language fluency and family power.

In discussing these issues, Teresia had suggested I consider the resonances of the Māori term "whakapapa . . . understood as genealogy but more literally as a process of layering. In that sense, whakapapa is not exclusively about familial or biological descent, but can be about any historical relationship." Citing Aroha Harris' 2009 work on the importance of the "whakapapa of experience" for urban Māori who left their marae-based communities during World War II, she noted that, "it wasn't just your iwi affiliation that was important, but which industry you worked in, which boarding house you lived in, which sports club you played for, etcetera" (pers. comm., 2014). These locations of experience and affiliation are also locations of knowledge production; whose stories you hear; who you come to feel is related to you and how.

Genealogies of Knowledge and Relation

Moʻokūʻauhau's expansiveness and emphasis on relation is in sharp contrast with ideas about "race" and "blood" imported from the continental United States, where they have been, and still are, used to undermine the sovereignty and existence of the native nations of Turtle Island. I credit early conversations with J. Kēhaulani Kauanui (2008) as she worked on the project that would culminate in her book *Hawaiian Blood: Colonialism and the Politics of Sovereignty and Indigeneity*, in sparking my thinking about genealogy as metaphor and practice. Mainstream Euro-American ideas about genealogy often associate it with linearity, which is one-dimensional, or they recognize the multiple possibilities within genealogical narratives but discount this as somehow illegitimate because of the "picking and choosing" of naming one's ancestors, often in the service of linking to famous historical figures. Genealogy is never one-dimensional; it is always strategic, social and interactive, while at the same time deeply grounded in actual relations of kinship and ancestry (overlapping but non-identical categories).

Kauanui's book documents in detail the terrible consequences for Hawaiians of the importation and implementation of ideas about the measurement of "blood" quantum that overshadowed Hawaiian cultural frameworks of relatedness. When I teach introductory indigenous studies classes I try to explain to students immersed in the ideas of U.S. racialization and fractionalization about the intentionally deadly consequences of blood quantum ideologies practiced by colonial governmental entities and internalized by various indigenous peoples.

In the practice's crude terms an "Indian" and a non-Indian produce a ½ Indian; a half-Indian plus a non-Indian produces a ¼ Indian and so on down a diminishing line, whose fractions are used by those opposed to Indian nations' sovereignty and rights to undermine those nations and peoples. These fractions are the bedrock of the fiction of the "vanishing Indian." In contrast, there is no such concept of "half-citizenship," though dual or multiple citizenships are possible. The 2013 mainstream media narratives about the court struggle of Cherokee citizen and U.S. military veteran, Dusten Brown, contesting the illegal adoption of his daughter Veronica repeatedly described him as only having a tiny fraction of "Cherokee blood" and his daughter, born of a non-Cherokee mother, as having even less. This is a blatant attempt to delegitimize Brown's right to the protections of the Indian Child Welfare Act enacted by the U.S. Congress for exactly this reason, to help stem the flood of Indian children being removed from their families and communities and given to others.

In contrast to this fractionalization, traditional Hawaiian notions of genealogy are both bilateral, recognizing both mothers and fathers (and there could be more than one genealogical father), and inclusive. A Hawaiian plus a non-Hawaiian produces a Hawaiian child who could birth their own child with a non-Hawaiian and continue to have another Hawaiian child. To riff on the classic "turtle story" of the world, it is Hawaiian all the way down. It may be other things as well, but those heritages are additive, not inherently diluting. There may be conflicting ideas about who and what adds to the mana (power) of genealogical lines, but these ideas traditionally do not revolve around a Hawaiian/non-Hawaiian distinction but rather on hierarchies among Hawaiians. Genealogy connects Hawaiians to place as well as people; the ultimate Hawaiian genealogy includes nonhuman life forms as well as things seen as inanimate in Western epistemologies. Kalo, the sustaining food of the Kānaka Maoli, is also our sibling. Destruction of land and water resources constitutes destruction of kinship relationships and sites of historical memory and contemporary knowledge production.

Kuleana and Moʻolelo

Kuleana is a difficult concept to convey in English, with its multiple connotations of care, responsibility, and authority. It entails what you have the right to do, what you are spiritually impelled to do, and what is none of your business. Kuleana affects the stories we tell; the stories we hear shape our knowledge of our kuleana.

I currently teach at a very small liberal arts college in upstate New York located on Cayuga land in the territory of the Haudenosaunee/Six Nations/ Iroquois Confederacy. When I first arrived for my interview for the position, the college van drove from the Rochester airport through a late night sea of red, white, and blue signs put up by the white property owners who call themselves "Upstate Citizens for Equality," proclaiming, "No Sovereign Nation. No Cayuga land claim." Though I found the signs chilling, they were also paradoxically a form of recognition of contemporary Cayuga and general Indian existence even as they attempted to negate it. The myth of the "vanishing Indian" is in some ways undercut by the visibility of upstate New York struggles about Indian gaming, taxation, and land claims. Living here these past eight years has immersed me in learning about the struggles and knowledges of this locale.

Wells College has some history of acknowledging its relation to Cayuga land, such as an annual commemoration of Sullivan's burning of the crops during the Revolutionary War and a festival celebrating Cayuga and Haudenosaunee culture; faculty who helped create a land base for the dispossessed Cayuga Nation in the form of a farm deeded to them and supported by students and faculty; and, developing a minor in First Nations and Indigenous Studies orienting students to local and global indigenous struggles. Thus, as an educational entity in this area we stand somewhere between Syracuse University and Cornell University. Whereas, Syracuse University publicly acknowledges its relation and debt to the Onondaga Nation on whose land it sits, and offers full scholarships to any admitted Haudenosaunee students as part of its "Haudenosaunee Promise," Cornell University makes no public institutional acknowledgment of its relationship to the Cayuga, or the Confederacy, even though it is a land grant institution. The American Indian and Indigenous Studies program at Cornell struggles to make indigenous intellectual and political issues legible to the rest of the university even as it carries forward its own rich history of scholarship and activism. Jolene Rickard, AIISP director, artist, and visual historian, created a site-specific installation for the "Lines of Control" (2012) exhibition at Cornell's Johnson Art Museum, where everyday street signs were transformed and mapped by Cayuga language and overlaid with images of historical struggle. Her work literally and figuratively remapped the space of Cornell and upstate New York.

What stories do we need to tell to be responsible to place and people? What knowledges do we need to learn and pass on? These are fundamental questions raised within indigenous studies, settler colonial studies, comparative ethnic studies, but often not between these knowledge communities. The particularities of this landscape and its accompanying issues have pushed me to think further about the genealogy of knowledge over the years I have lived here: who knows whom, who is exposed to whom, and in what contexts—moʻokuʻauhau, moʻolelo, and kuleana. What were we born; what will we become; what stories are we responsible to tell?

References

Act of War: The Overthrow of the Hawaiian Nation. 1993. Directed by Puhipau. Hawaiʻi: Nā Maka o ka ʻĀina.

Bonura, Sandra, and Sally Witmer. 2013. "Lydia K. Aholo—Her Story: Recovering the Lost Voice." *Hawaiian Journal of History* 47:103–145.

Christian, Barbara. 1987. "The Race for Theory." *Cultural Critique* 6 (Spring): 51–63.

Crossing the Rainbow Bridge: Our Story. 2001. Directed by Adrian Carrizales, Kat High, and Darryl Wilson. Topanga: Giveaway Songs Productions.

Demos, John. 2014. *The Heathen School: A Story of Hope and Betrayal in the Age of the Early Republic*. New York: Knopf.

Hall, Lisa Kahaleole. 2009. "Navigating Our Own "Sea of Islands": Remapping a Theoretical Space for Hawaiian Women and Indigenous Feminism." *Wicazo Sa Review* 24, no. 2:15–38.

———. 2015. "Which of These Things Is Not Like the Other: Hawaiians and Other Pacific Islanders Are Not Asian Americans, and All Pacific Islanders Are Not Hawaiian." *American Quarterly* 67, no. 3:727–747.

Harris, Aroha. 2009. "'Sharing Our Differences Together': Whakapapa of Experience in Post-war Auckland." Presentation, National Indigenous Studies Conference, Canberra, Australia, October 1.

Kauanui, J. Kēhaulani, 2008. *Hawaiian Blood: Colonialism and the Politics of Sovereignty and Indigeneity*. Durham, NC: Duke University Press.

Kimura, Larry. 1983. "Native Hawaiian Culture." In *Native Hawaiians Study Commission, Report on the Culture, Needs and Concerns of Native Hawaiians*, vol. II. Honolulu: Native Hawaiians Study Commission, pp. 182–184.

King, Thomas. 2008. *The Truth About Stories*. Minneapolis: University of Minnesota Press.

Kohala Center Media Release. 2012. "Puana Ka Ike: Brown Shares Stories of Moʻo." http://www.hawaii247.com/2012/02/21/puana-ka-ike-brown-shares-stories-of -moo/.

ʻŌlelo TV. 2014. " DOI hearings." http://www.olelo.org/recognition/.

Peek, Michelle. 2013. "Kinship Flows in Brandy Nālani McDougall's *The Salt-Wind/Ka Makani Paʻakai.*" *Feminist Review* 103:80.

Pukui, Mary Kawena. 1983. *ʻŌlelo Noʻeau: Hawaiian Proverbs and Poetical Sayings.* Honolulu: Bishop Museum Press.

Silva, Noenoe. 2004a. *Aloha Betrayed: Native Hawaiian Resistance to American Colonialism.* Durham, NC: Duke University Press.

———. 2004b. "I Kū Mau Mau: How Kanaka Maoli Tried To Sustain National Identity Within the United States Political System." *American Studies* 45, no. 3:9–31.

Simpson, Leanne. 2014. "RBC Taylor Emerging Writer Award Leanne Simpson on the Significance of Storytelling." Interview by CBC Canada Writes, June 20. https://web.archive.org/web/20150424185103/http://www.cbc.ca/books/canadawrites/2014/06/rbc-taylor-emerging-writer-award-leanne-simpson-on-the-significance-of-storytelling.html.

Takaki, Ronald. 1984. *Pau Hana: Plantation Life and Labor in Hawaii, 1835–1920.* Honolulu: University of Hawaiʻi Press.

9

MOʻOKŪʻAUHAU AS METHODOLOGY

Sailing into the Future, Guided by the Past

NĀLANI WILSON-HOKOWHITU

> I go by the moons
> expectant
> feeling in the throat
> for the chanter.
>
> *Trask,* Light in the Crevice Never Seen

The full moon was our only light. We had been at sea sailing between Rapa Nui (Easter Island) and Tahiti for several weeks so our connections to the land and ocean had shifted. I was on watch, steering, when I felt the presence of a woman in the moon. In that moment, under the radiant, intensity of the moonlight, a vision came into my mind of Kalamaʻula, Molokaʻi. It was my grandmother's Hawaiian homestead and I was working in the garden. As I reflect on this story, I still cannot give the presence that I felt in the moon a name. Was it Grandma Einei? Was it Hina, Mother of Molokaʻi? Or Hina-nui-te-araara, who resides in the moon and watches over travelers?[1] Were these my imaginings, or was this a message of guidance from my ancestors of recent and distant past, their continuity alive and well, directing my life's journey? After sailing with the double-hulled canoe, *Hōkūleʻa*, on the Voyage to Rapa Nui, the vision that I saw in the middle of the open ocean materalized and I moved to Kalamaʻula, Molokaʻi, to help my cousin, Manuwai, take care of our grandmother's Hawaiian homestead.[2]

I open with this deeply personal story as an embodiment of moʻokūʻauhau as methodology. This story marks one of many pivotal moments when nā kūpuna (our ancestors) offered their support and guidance. Within the quest of (re)searching, questioning, and asking, we are not alone. This is my interpretation of moʻokūʻauhau as methodology. The last line in Haunani-Kay Trask's poem, "I go by the moons," is powerful, because as Kānaka Maoli we are guided by our ancestors who are embodied in the natural world and present within our being. This epistemological belief and understanding comes with a great kuleana (responsibility) to make a contribution to the larger good, to the broader community of Kānaka Maoli and to our islands, and the Earth. *Expectant, feeling in the throat for the chanter*, we know that the time will come for us to stand tall and proud, to oli (chant) our moʻokūʻauhau, our connections, our perspectives, and our stories.

This chapter engages moʻokūʻauhau as methodology in multiple ways by interweaving four core values of ʻapo (acceptance), hoʻololi (transformation), hoʻonui (expansion), and lōkahi (unity).[3] Sailing into the future guided by the past articulates moʻokūʻauhau as guidance drawing upon personal stories from the canoe *Hōkūleʻa* and the Hawaiian diaspora. At the heart of the writing is a call for acceptance and openness. As Kānaka of the new millennium, we are all so incredibly diverse, yet we are bound together by our shared moʻokūʻauhau. When we go far enough back into our geneaologies and the Kumulipo we find that we are all a part of the beginnings of existence and that our relations extend far beyond our indigeneity and our human bonds to the Earth, Sky, Stars, Sun, Moon, Wind, Water, Trees, Ocean, Rocks, and into all and everything. This profound consciousness can at times be sidelined by the very task that we are striving to accomplish, like the writing of a methodology section! So ironically our research and writing has the potential to both separate us and, with concious clarity, connect us to the essence of our being. As a diasporic Hawaiian, I have grown to accept my lived experiences and to hoʻololi (transform) this consciousness, to hoʻonui (expand), moving through feelings of longing and discomfort so that growth can occur.

As Kānaka we have a shared indigenous connection to the Hawaiian archipelago. For some we follow in the footsteps of our ancestors or devote our lives to specific practices such as activism, education, sovereignty, wayfinding, celestial navigation, hula, taro cultivation, surfing, paddling, and in the multitude of ways that we thrive in these modern times. Within these practices and beyond, guidance happens both physically and metaphysically. Having lived away from the Hawaiian Islands for over a decade, spirit has sustained my relationship with nā kūpuna and ka piko o Hawaiʻi, or Hawaiʻi as a central focus of my life's work and purpose as a contemporary Kanaka voyager and scholar of the canoe *Hōkūleʻa*.[4]

Being guided by the past can also be fueled through knowledge gained about historical atrocities, oppression, and our colonial histories of abuse and exploitation. Learning about and understanding the past can be painful but powerful. Drawing upon voyaging as a metaphor, adversity is like the wind. We can use it to harness energy, to focus our sail plan into the future with consciousness and to move forward, blazing ahead. So, it is with the past that we chart our course to sail into the future, knowing that unity is vital to our progression as Kānaka Maoli, Pacific peoples, Indigenous peoples, and as humans on the Earth.

ʻApo (Acceptance)

How do we move forward into a more loving, peaceful future? Acceptance of one another and of our complexities and contradictions as beings on this Earth is a beautiful place to start. We are indigenous/non-indigenous, traditional/contemporary, urban/rural, wanderer/settler, warrior/healer, rooted/flying, reaching, striving, and on the move. We have the capacity to deeply connect to the Earth and place, while in another juxtaposing moment we are able to surf across the globe through cyberspace. How do these skills relate? They are both about connection, connections to that which is greater than one's self and connections to one another. We are living and thriving in very different landscapes, cultures, spaces, places, and realities. We are neither one nor the other; we are simultaneously all of these attributes and energies. We call upon each strength and skill with fluidity and purpose from one moment to the next.

With guidance from our kūpuna we can begin the journey to fulfill our kuleana, always searching, questioning, and discovering. It is a tremendously humbling process. At times our research can feel overwhelming and discombobulating. When feelings of doubt or fear arise, I return to the connections and teachings that have been nurtured along this expansive journey of life. For example, while facilitating this collection and living in Canada, I felt incredibly distant from, yet simultaneously connected to, the contributors. Geographically we were all over the globe, in Canada, Hawaiʻi, Aotearoa, Minnesota, and New York, but via cyberspace we could dialogue on Skype or correspond on Facebook and by email. One day while in the Mill Creek Ravine near our home, I stopped with my children to listen to the birds in the trees overhead. It was mid-winter and the earth was frozen, white with snow. As I looked up into this one tree, the wind began to blow, at first moving the branches, and then I saw all the trees in the forest swaying in flowing unison likes waves in the ocean. I realized in that amazing teaching moment that our kūpuna are like the wind and we are the trees, moving and working together. I learned that trees speak when moved by the wind.

Acceptance leads to appreciation. Appreciation enables clarity and with clarity we can strive to make our research and lives more abundant. Simply accepting who we are and where we are in our lives facilitates appreciation. As academics, we are so fortunate to have the privilege to learn, grow, and expand. It is vital to realize the inherent abundance within the simple pleasure of being able to write and create or read and ingest new ideas. Ideally these new ideas, or perhaps ancient ideas revisited, can be transformative. This learning can at times be uncomfortable and take us out of our comfort zones. When this happens embrace transition, because it is in these painful moments that we are growing!

Hoʻololi (Transformation)

Imagine the tree, roots deep into the earth and reaching toward the sky. It is grounded in the dark abundance of the soil while simultaneously stretching toward the sun. The tree has the potential to transform into a canoe, a carving, or the very paper upon which these words are written. Tree has the potential to carry culture and embody spirit in many different forms. If we are like the tree, imagine our capacity to transform. Upon considering research, how can we make our work transformative, innovative, and inspirational? Let us draw upon the canoe *Hōkūleʻa* and the academic discourses and waves that the canoe has had to ride as an example:

> One exceptionally clear night I stayed up quite late, star chart in hand, memorizing the stars and their relative positions. When I finally went to sleep, I dreamed of stars, and my attention was attracted to Arcturus. It appeared to grow larger and brighter, so brilliant that I awoke. I turned on my reading light and wrote "Hōkūleʻa." The next morning, I saw the notation and immediately recognized it as a fitting name for the canoe. As a zenith star for Hawaiʻi, it would indeed be a star of gladness if it led to landfall. (Herb Kāne cited by Low 2000, 25)

Hōkūleʻa rode the wave of social change in the Pacific and arrived in the islands of our ancient homeland with an unforeseen impact. Upon re-visiting and re-reading texts written about the canoe *Hōkūleʻa*, I felt moved by the quote above because I believe that it reveals the presence of nā kūpuna, nā ʻaumākua and the power of our Kanaka Maoli moʻokūʻauhau to connect us, if we are open to the dreams and visions that our ancestors plant like seeds in our conscious and subconscious. Kāne describes how in a dream state the zenith star over the Hawaiian Islands, the star called *Hōkūleʻa*, appeared to grow larger and brighter, so brilliant that he roused from a subconscious state into consciousness. A name that comes in this way is called inoa pō (name in the night) and is considered a gift from the ancestors. In reading this story, I got chills and a feeling that the vision of *Hōkūleʻa*, meaning "star of gladness," growing larger and brighter was a hōʻailona (sign)[5] from the ancestors about the mana that the canoe would have in revitalizing an appreciation and pride in our Kanaka Maoli and Pacific Islands heritage, culture, and identity.[6]

Herb Kāne described a conversation he had with Ben Finney in 1973 about how the creation of the canoe might strengthen Pacific Islanders' pride in our rich heritage (Kāne 1976). The founders of the PVS and creators of the *Hōkūleʻa* set out to prove that Polynesians sailed and navigated with the utmost intention, but they could not have known what an immense impact this would have on contemporary Hawaiian and Pacific peoples. I interpret the image that Kāne describes in his dream of the star *Hōkūleʻa* growing larger and brighter to represent the way in which the canoe *Hōkūleʻa* would ignite an energy difficult to articulate, yet capable of connecting people of the Pacific to one another and to ourselves, to our ancient origins, ancestors, and our own rich moʻokūʻauhau as Kānaka Maoli.

The retelling of this story about the double-hulled sailing canoe *Hōkūleʻa* focuses on my belief in the prophecy of Kāne's dream and the power of the canoe to re-story Polynesian migration, thus *restoring* Kanaka Maoli perceptions of ourselves in a modern and Indigenous present where both co-exist and thrive. Briefly considering the context and challenges that Kānaka have endured for several centuries, puts into perspective why celebrating the canoe, named after the star of gladness, and its amazing capacities has had such a vast impact.

The canoe *Hōkūleʻa* fueled a revival of transpacific non-instrumental navigation and re-instilled Pacific people with a feeling of pride, identity, and connection in the twentieth century. Western dominance surrounding disempowering discourses about Pacific peoples' unintentional arrival to our islands was so strong that it actually took the voice and pursuit of another Western male to initially challenge these racist assumptions. The research and experimental archaeology of Ben Finney that began as early as 1965 out of the University of California at Santa Barbara, and eventually led to the construction of a replica of a double-hulled deep sea sailing canoe, the *Hōkūleʻa*, has been invaluable to the people of the Pacific region (Finney 1976, 1977, 1979, 1985, 1992, 1994, 2003, 2006a, 2006b). Three men, an academic, Ben Finney; an artist, Herb Kāne; and a sailor, Tommy Holmes, envisioned, researched, designed, engineered, and fundraised for the creation of the *Hōkūleʻa*; but it was the support and volunteer hours of hundreds of Kānaka Maoli and others that made the canoe come to life.

Moʻokūʻauhau as methodology is about honing in on our Indigenous and Pacific strengths and attributes while prioritizing our epistmologies and ontologies within and throughout the research process. Looking deep within our naʻau (gut) to make decisions that are pono (right/balanced), and trusting the guidance of our ancestors are the first steps toward conducting transformative work. The research project that created the canoe transformed as more Kānaka got involved in the life of *Hōkūleʻa* and, thus, the canoe has developed a life of its own that has persevered beyond the university project. This has happened in several ways: for example, the canoe community began planting koa trees to reforest our depleted native ecosystems, and visited the Northwestern Hawaiian Islands to bring attention to the human impact of waste and plastics floating to shore and entrapping seabirds and ocean animals like the monk seal. Hula hālau began composing oli (chants) to welcome the canoe home and developing protocol when sending the canoe off to sea. Thoughout the past forty years networks across the globe have been forged due to the voyages of the *Hōkūleʻa*. So, upon delving into your own research project, ask yourself, how can your research project develop a life of its own beyond words on paper? How can the work that we do bring people together and inspire others to create and dream?

Hoʻonui (Expansion)

The canoe *Hōkūleʻa* serves as an excellent example of all the core values highlighted within this chapter. This section will focus on the expansive nature of the *Hōkūleʻa*, which has sailed half way around the globe—including in the Atlantic Ocean along the east coast of the United States—in its quest to circumnavigate the earth to raise awareness about the fragility of our planet. Hoʻonui, or expansion, is a term that I am using to describe the sensation of moving out of your comfort zone with purpose and clear intention.

After completing my doctoral degree five years ago, I returned to Hawaiʻi to mahalo the women from *Hōkūleʻa* that I had interviewed for the thesis project that focused on the lived experiences of Kanaka Maoli women from the canoe. Each woman shared their thoughts about the proposed worldwide voyage. They described the varying perspectives on whether *Hōkūleʻa* should leave the Pacific Ocean. Since *Hōkūleʻa* set sail, she has just kept sailing! The idea that the canoe should remain in Pacific waters is interesting, and perhaps the worldwide voyage created feelings of discomfort and fear for the safety of our beloved canoe. The voyage now represents hoʻonui, taking Herb Kāne's dream of the star of gladness growing brighter and brighter and Ben Finney's experimental archaeology into realms unimaginable in the 1970s!

Much like the research journey, or a voyage over the open ocean, there will be challenges, barriers, and obstacles that are difficult. Overcoming challenges is a way to hoʻonui. The challenges that we might experience in our research journey might come from the lack of understanding and comprehension from our supervisors or peers, especially when working away from the Hawaiian Islands or outside of Hawaiian or Indigenous studies faculties; yet, it is vital to persevere.

As an example, *Hōkūleʻa* kept sailing through the academic authenticity debates that transpired following the initial successful voyages of the canoe and the cultural revival of the '70s and '80s. In Hawaiʻi, anthropologists such as Jocelyn Linnekin (2000) and Roger Keesing (1991, 2000) began debating the authenticity of our present Indigeneity, as Kānaka Maoli and Pacific peoples. By the turn of the millennium, activist and academic leader, Haunani-Kay Trask (2000) challenged Linnekin and Keesing, creating clashing views on controversial issues in anthropology. During this time, Ben Finney (2000) wrote about the "Sin at Awarua," bringing to light in descriptive detail the fusion of cultural revival practices and the juxtapositioning of contemporary conflicts surrounding the arrival of *Hōkūleʻa* at Taputapuatea on the island of Raʻiātea, in the Tahitian Island archipelago. These examples offer a mere glimpse at a few challenges and the complexity of our contemporary Indigenous and academic conversations that have the potential to influence present and future discourses. It is for this reason that it is powerful to harness adversity as fuel for continued innovation as Indigenous peoples and to overcome the obstacles that seek to sidetrack our visions.

Sailing into the future, guided by the past, represents the way in which we negotiate our traditional and contemporary realities. We sail into the future using the resources that will best suit our intentions. For academics the use of technology, literature, the Internet, and the multiplicity of resources available to help us explore research topics with the potential to lift up our people while honoring our ancestors are examples of "sailing into the future, guided by the past." Again, the complexity of *Hōkūleʻa*, our mama canoe, offers an excellent example. *Hōkūleʻa*'s double hulls are made from fiberglass and the voyagers use solar panels, harnessing alternative energy to stay in touch with schools and the greater public while sailing. The practice of wayfinding and voyaging are both ancient and transforming, sailing into the future while remaining deeply connected to ancestral vision and guidance.

These complexities can stimulate difficult decisions and conversations, which can happen on paper within academic texts or in person. Yet, they have the capacity to hoʻonui our thinking and to encourage others to think and feel more openly. These moments of tension are opportunities for growth and connection. Even when there are disagreements, there is still connection. The disagreements help us to delve deeply into our own beliefs and opinions. However, it is helpful to return to compassion and understanding for continued growth.

Lōkahi (Unity)

Connectedness. If there is one word that I want you to remember from this chapter it is our connectedness. The word that I use to express our profound connectedness is moʻokūʻauhau. Literally translated into the English language moʻokūʻauhau means genealogy. Moʻo in ʻōlelo Hawaiʻi means succession, kū is the god of war (or it can also mean steadfast), and ʻauhau is literally the femur bone. When strung together moʻokūʻauhau refers to our Kanaka Maoli ancestry. Included within this genealogical lineage are nā akua, nā ʻaumakua, nā kūpuna, our ancestors both living and in spirit. Our relations are embodied within everything that exists. The Kumulipo, our creation chant, recites these interconnections and our relationships with each other extending from and beyond the natural world.

Upon contemplation of moʻokūʻauhau, I feel as though the most vital thread is connectedness. It is our connectedness to the light and energy within and extending into all things—past, present, and future. This collective consciousness has the power and capacity to heal our world and to propel us into a more sustainable, peaceful, and loving future. *Hōkūleʻa* is leading on this path toward our global connection, riding this wave of consciousness with an utmost clarity that is truly beautiful to witness. The intention to foster a more sustainable world has mana and as the canoe reaches more and more shores on its journey to circumnavigate the globe, the intention grows stronger.

I find that it has been my geographical separation from Hawaiʻi nei and feelings of dislocation, which have ironically enabled me to more profoundly understand the importance of connection, both indigenous and global. As a global citizen, who has immigrated and lived in several countries, including Argentina, Aotearoa (New Zealand), Canada, and the United States, I have simultaneously gained awareness of what my Indigeneity means. In this quest, I have returned to spirit, and our connectedness to all beings, in particular the Earth, Sky, and Ocean.

Epeli Hauʻofaʻs essay entitled, "Our Sea of Islands," transformed and expanded our thinking about the Pacific region. Within the growing discipline of Pacific Islands studies, the idea that our islands are not isolated and remote, but rather that we are connected by the Pacific Ocean, reconfigured our theorizing about Pacific spaces, places, and peoples. The essay sought to refresh our thinking about ourselves as Pacific Islanders, and our geographies, to empower a consciousness of connectedness and unity (Hauʻofa 1993, 1994, 2000a, 2000b). *Hōkūleʻa* is forging the same intention, but instead of "Our Sea of Islands" the canoe is sailing for "Our Island Earth,"

Whether circumnavigating the globe on the canoe *Hōkūleʻa*, or surfing the Internet, our world is becoming more and more interconnected.

What role does Indigenous studies play in this monumental quest? When we consider Indigenous studies over the decades, we find that initially Western imperialism sought to either erase Indigeneity from the globe or, at best, assimilate Indigenous cultures and epistemologies into Western notions of being. Within the academy, initially all things Indigenous were spoken about as historical, as existing in the past.

Hōkūleʻa's worldwide voyage is exciting because it launches our consciousness out of the past, beyond the present, and into the future. The voyage challenges us to rethink and reframe our collective consciousness about the world as an island in the universe, to propel us into a better future. This is a fantastic example of Indigenous innovation and a very exciting time: *Hōkūleʻa*'s worldwide voyage forges our futurity in complex, seemingly contradictory ways. For example, we see how Indigeneity and global citizenship cán co-exist. In this instance, our island knowledge is metaphorical, of the earth as an island in the universe with limited resources and a place that we must all share and take care of. The leaders of the canoe voyage clearly state that they do not intend to change the world, but that they are striving to create a network of people that will.

Hopena (Conclusion)

Sailing into the future, guided by the past, we honor our moʻokūʻauhau. The intention of this chapter, as well as the entire collection, is that moʻokūʻauhau will reemerge as a central focus in our lives as contemporary Kānaka ʻŌiwi. Our collective represents a growing network of scholars committed to creating social, political, and epistemological change. Like the "star of gladness" growing brighter and stronger, my intention is that in time we will see emancipatory differences as a result of our writing. Moʻokūʻauhau rejects blood quantum and colonial imbued definitions of our indigenity (Kauanui 2008). I offer the themes of acceptance, transformation, expansion, and unity as inspiration. In this chapter, I do not intend to profess to "end all truths," but rather, to humbly offer guidance toward our potential abundance, as researchers and people. We continue to honor our moʻokūʻauhau in many different ways, in all the roles that we fulfill, in the very essence of our being. We are our kūpuna.

Notes

Epigraph. Trask, *Light in the Crevice Never Seen*, 96.

1.   In Tahiti, Hina is remembered as the daughter of Ātea and Hotu. She is known for her voyage of discovery to Aotearoa (New Zealand) accompanied by her brother, Rū. They departed from Motu-tapu in Raʻiātea through Te-ara-o Hina

("the passage of Hina") and ventured south across the Pacific. In this story Hina is Hina-faʻauru-vaʻa, or "Hina the canoe pilot" (Henry 1995, 4). After exploring several islands in Polynesia, Hina embarked upon an even greater voyage. On the night of the full moon, just as the moon met the horizon, she set sail to visit it. Upon arriving she let her canoe drift away and decided never to return to the earth. From the moon, she watches over travelers at night, and in this manifestation is called Hina-nui-te-araara ("Great Hina the watchwoman").

2. For more on Molokaʻi, voyaging, and methodology see Wilson (2004, 2005, 2008a, 2008b, 2008c, 2011), and Wilson-Hokowhitu (2012).

3. I would like to humbly acknowledge one of my kumu (teachers), Jocelyn, who inspired the themes of this chapter through our practice of quieting the mind.

4. For more on spirit and diaspora methodologies see Dillard, "When the Ground Is Black, the Ground Is Fertile" (2008).

5. For more on inoa pō and hōʻailona see Pūkui, Haertig, and Lee, *Nānā I Ke Kumu, Look to the Source* (1972).

6. For more about the Hawaiian Renaissance see Kanahele, *Hawaiian Renaissance* (1982).

References

Beckwith, Martha. 1951. *The Kumulipo*. Chicago: University of Chicago Press.

Dillard, C. 2008. "When the Ground Is Black, the Ground Is Fertile: Exploring Feminist Epistemology and Healing Methodologies of the Spirit." In *Handbook of Critical and Indigenous Methodologies*, edited by N. Denzin, Y. Lincoln, and L. T. Smith. Thousand Oaks: Sage Publishing.

Finney, Ben. 1992. *From Sea To Space*. Palmerston North: Massey University Publisher.

———. 1979. *Hokuleʻa: The Way to Tahiti*. New York: Dodd, Mead.

———. 1991. "Myth, Experiment and the Reinvention of Polynesian Voyaging." *American Anthropologist* 93(2): 383–404.

———. 2006a. "Ocean sailing canoes." In *Vaka Moana: Voyages of the Ancestors*, edited by K. R. Howe. Auckland: David Bateman.

———, ed. 1976. *Pacific Navigation and Voyaging*. Wellington: The Polynesian Society.

———. 2006b. "Renaissance." In *Vaka Moana: Voyages of the Ancestors*, edited by K. R. Howe. Auckland: David Bateman Ltd.

———. 2003. *Sailing in the Wake of the Ancestors: Reviving Polynesian Voyaging*. Honolulu: Bishop Museum Press.

———. 2000. "The Sin at Awarua." In *Voyaging Through the Contemporary Pacific*, edited by D. Hanlon, and G. White. Lanham: Rowman & Littlefield Publishers, Inc.

———. 1994. *Voyage of Rediscovery: A Cultural Odyssey Through Polynesia*. Berkley: University of California Press.

———. 1977. "Voyaging Canoes and the Settlement of Polynesia." *Science* 196: 1277–1285.

Finney, Ben, and Sam Low. 2006. "Navigation." In *Vaka Moana: Voyages of the Ancestors*, edited by K. R. Howe. Auckland: David Bateman, Ltd.

Goodyear-Kaʻopua, Jennifer. 2005. "Kū i ka Māna: Building Community and Nation Through Contemporary Hawaiian Schooling." Unpublished doctoral diss., University of California, Santa Cruz.

Hauʻofa, Epeli. 2000b. "The Ocean in Us." In *Voyaging Through the Contemporary Pacific*, edited by D. Hanlon, and G. White. Lanham: Rowman & Littlefield.

———. 1993. "Our Sea of Islands." In *A New Oceania, Rediscovering Our Sea of Islands*, edited by E. Waddell, V. Naidu, and E. Hauʻofa. Suva: University of the South Pacific.

———. 1994. "Our Sea of Islands." *The Contemporary Pacific* 6(1): 148–161.

———. 2000a. "Pasts to Remember." In *Remembering Pacific Pasts*, edited by R. Borofsky, 453–469. Honolulu: University of Hawaiʻi Press.

Henry, Teuira. 1928. *Ancient Tahiti*. Honolulu: Bulletin no. 48 of the Bernice Pauahi Bishop Museum.

———. 1995. *Voyaging Chiefs of Havaiʻi*. Honolulu: Kalamakū Press.

Kanahele, George. 1982. *Hawaiian Renaissance*. Honolulu: Project WAIAHA.

———. 1986. *Kū Kanaka: Stand Tall—A Search for Hawaiian Values*. Honolulu: University of Hawaiʻi Press.

Kauanui, J. Kēhaulani. 2008. *Hawaiian Blood-Colonialism and the Politics of Sovereignty and Indigeneity*. Durham: Duke University Press.

Low, Sam. 2000. "Voyages of Awakening." *Hana Hou*, vol 3, no 1, 21–31.

Meyer, Manulani. 2003. *Hoʻoulu*. Honolulu: ʻAi Pohakū Press.

———. 2008. "Indigenous and authentic: Hawaiian epistemology and the triangulation of meaning." In *Critical and Indigenous Methodologies*, edited by N. Denzin, Y. Lincoln, and L. Smith, 217–232. Thousand Oaks: Sage Publications.

Pukui, Mary Kawena. 1983. *ʻŌlelo Noʻeau: Hawaiian Proverbs and Poetical Sayings*. Honoulu: Bishop Museum Press.

Pukui, M., E. Haertig, and C. Lee. 1972. *Nānā I Ke Kumu, Look to the Source*, vol. I. Honolulu: Hui Hānai.

Smith, Linda. 1999. *Decolonizing Methodologies: Research and Indigenous Peoples*. Dunedin: University of Otago Press/Zed Books.

Trask, Haunani-Kay. 1994. *Light in the Crevice Never Seen*. Corvallis, OR: CALYX Books.

Wilson, K. L. Nālani. 2011. "Nā Moʻokūʻauhau Holowaʻa: Native Hawaiian Women's Stories of the Voyaging Canoe *Hōkūleʻa*." Doctoral thesis, University of Otago, Dunedin, New Zealand.

———. 2008a. "Nā Wāhine Kanaka Maoli Holowaʻa: Native Hawaiian Women Voyagers." *International Journal of Maritime History* 20, no. 2: 307–324.

———. 2004. "Nā Wāhine Piko o Molokaʻi: Pacific Women's Connections to Place." Unpublished Master's thesis, Centre of Pacific Islands Studies, University of Hawaiʻi, Mānoa.

———. 2005. "View from the Mountain: Molokaʻi nui a Hina." *Junctures*, 31–46.

Wilson, Nālani. 2008c. "Reflection on Molokaʻi nui a Hina." In *Indigenous Educational Models for Contemporary Practice*, edited by M. Ah Nee-Benham, 194–198. New York: Routledge.

———. 2008b. "A Waka Ama Journey: Reflections on Outrigger Canoe Paddling as a Medium for Epistemological Adventuring." *Pathways: The Ontario Journal of Outdoor Education* 21, no. 1: 19–23.

Wilson-Hokowhitu, Nālani 2012. "He Pukoa Kani ʻaina: Kanaka Maoli Approaches to Moʻokūʻauhau as Methodology." *AlterNative: An International Journal of Indigenous Peoples* 8, no. 2.

About the Contributors

Hōkūlani K. Aikau is Kanaka ʻŌiwi Hawaiʻi and an associate professor in the Divisions of Gender and Ethnic Studies at the University of Utah. She is the author of *A Chosen People, a Promised Land: Mormonism and Race in Hawaiʻi* (2012), which examines the intersections of race, religion, and Native Hawaiian identity in the Church of Jesus Christ of Latter-day Saints in Hawaiʻi. She worked with Kākoʻo ʻŌiwi, a Native Hawaiian nonprofit organization restoring loʻi kalo (wetland taro farming) in the ahupuaʻa of Heʻeʻia on the island of Oʻahu. She is also mom to Sanoe, ʻĪmaikalani, and Hiʻilei.

Marie Alohalani Brown hails from Mākaha, Oʻahu, but her ʻŌiwi roots begin in Hoʻokena at the foot of Mauna Loa, Hawaiʻi. An assistant professor of religion at the University of Hawaiʻi, Mānoa, her areas of expertise include Hawaiian religion, belief narratives, historical treaties, and life writing, but also indigenous theories/methodologies for the study of religion and expressive culture, folklore studies, and translation studies. Her first book, *Facing the Spears of Change: The Life and Legacy of John Papa ʻĪʻī* (2016) won the Palapala Poʻokela award (2017) for Best Book on Hawaiian Language, Culture, and History.

Manulani Aluli Meyer writes, teaches, and works in the field of indigenous epistemology and its role in worldwide awakening. Dr. Aluli Meyer earned her doctorate from Harvard in 1998 on the topic of Hawaiian epistemology. She is a former associate professor of education at the University of Hawaiʻi, Hilo, and has recently returned to Oʻahu as the Director of Indigenous Education at the University of Hawaiʻi, West Oʻahu.

David A. Chang is a Kanaka Maoli historian of Hawaiʻi and the United States, focusing especially on the histories of Kānaka Maoli and other indigenous peoples. David is the author of *The World and All the Things upon It: Native Hawaiian Geographies of Exploration* (2016). The book draws on the rich archive of Hawaiian language sources to explore Hawaiians' perspectives on the nature of the nineteenth-century world and their place in it. He teaches in history and American Indian studies at the University of Minnesota.

Lisa Kahaleole Hall is Chair and associate professor in the women's and gender studies program and the National Endowment for the Humanities Preceptor in Women's Studies at Wells College in Aurora, New York. She also holds an appointment as courtesy associate professor in the American Indian program at Cornell University. Her previous publications include "'Hawaiian at Heart' and Other Fictions," in *The Contemporary Pacific*; "Navigating Our Own 'Sea of Islands': Remapping a Theoretical Space for Native Hawaiian Women and Indigenous Feminism," in *Wicazo Sa Review*; and "Strategies of Erasure: US Colonialism and Native Hawaiian Feminism," in *American Quarterly*.

kuʻualoha hoʻomanawanui is a Kanaka Maoli scholar, poet, artist, and mālama ʻāina advocate from Wailua Homesteads, Olohena, Kauaʻi. She is currently an associate professor of Hawaiian literature in the English Department at the University of Hawaiʻi, Mānoa. Her research and teaching specialties are Native Hawaiian literature, Pacific literatures, and indigenous rhetoric. She is the founding and current chief editor of *ʻŌiwi: A Native Hawaiian Journal*. Her first book, *Voices of Fire—Reweaving the Lei of Pele and Hiʻiaka Literature*, was published in 2014. She is currently developing Ka Ipu o Lono, a Native Hawaiian digital humanities resource of Hawaiian literature.

Kū Kahakalau is a Native Hawaiian educator, researcher, cultural practitioner, songwriter, and expert in Hawaiian language and culture. The first person to earn a doctorate in Indigenous education, Kahakalau is the founder of Hawaiʻi's first fully accredited K–12 Hawaiian-focused charter school and the designer of Pedagogy of Aloha, a successful, values- and place-based, culturally driven way of education. Kahakalau also created Basic Hawaiian, an innovative Hawaiian language and culture program balancing digital media and traditional, hands-on learning, and is currently developing EA Ecoversity, a Hawaiian-focused post-secondary program that transitions Indigenous youth to become thriving Kānaka and responsible global citizens.

Kalei Nuʻuhiwa was born and raised on the island of Maui. She has worked with the restoration of the island of Kahoʻolawe. She is a doctoral candidate at the University of Waikato and is the director of the Kūkeao & ʻAimalama projects for the Kamaʻaha Education Initiative. Her primary discipline is Papahulilani, the study of all aspects of the atmosphere, its phenology, energies, and cycles from a Hawaiian perspective.

ʻUmi Perkins is of the Apo, Makekau, and Kaʻaʻa clans of Lāhaina, Hāmākua, and Puna, Hawaiʻi. He received a PhD in political science from the University of Hawaiʻi, Mānoa, where he is the Mānoa Academy Scholar, teaching courses that are dual credit with Kamehameha Schools. He is also a lecturer at Windward Community College and the Matsunaga Institute for Peace and Conflict Resolution. His research focuses on Hawaiian land tenure. He has written for *The Nation, Hawaiʻi Review, Hūlili, Summit*, and contributed to the book *Native Nations: The Survival of Fourth World Peoples* (Charlton 2014).

Mehana Blaich Vaughan grew up where the moku of Heleleʻa and Koʻolau meet on the island of Kauaʻi. She is the mother of three young children and an assistant professor in the Department of Natural Resources and Environmental Management, Sea Grant College Program, and Hui ʻĀina Momona at the University of Hawaiʻi, Mānoa. Her research focuses on people's relationships with the places they care about, and she works to enhance community ability to mālama ʻāina (take care of the land). For over ten years, Mehana taught middle and high school and worked on developing place-based education programs with Kauaʻi community groups.

Nālani Wilson-Hokowhitu is a Kanaka ʻŌiwi global citizen, who has homelands across the world. Born in the Colorado Rocky Mountains, Nālani links her moʻokūʻauhau to Molokaʻi Nui a Hina and Kalapana, Hawaiʻi. She is a contemporary voyager and scholar of the canoe *Hōkūleʻa*, who has traveled and lived in many countries, including Argentina, Canada, and Aotearoa (New Zealand), where she presently resides. Nālani is an artist and academic, working as a research fellow at Te Kotahi Research Institute at the University of Waikato. Above all, she is a mother to Kalikookalani and Tai Kaʻaukai.

INDEX